Weekend Quilting with friends

Since this book is a beginner's guide to quilting, I thought it appropriate to talk about how my love of quilting began. . .

Back in the late 70's my husband, Fred, and I owned a sewing store in Port Charlotte, FL. He had been in the business for over 15 years when we married in 1976.

While I didn't sew much then, I soon caught the bug and started taking classes to learn more. My initial contribution to the store was decorating, writing newsletters, doing accounting and eventually teaching free-motion embroidery classes. In 1980, my love for Thread Painting led to my first book and our mail-order business, Speed Stitch. Because of Speed Stitch, we broadened our Instructor education through a nationwide event called S.M.A.R.T. Some of the invited instructors taught quilting, and my interest in learning to quilt started to bloom.

I have found that quilting starts for most of us because of friends or family. My first class was with my best friend, Patti Lee. We went to an all-day class in a lady's home about 50 miles away. We both made the same throw quilt ---- "A Trip Around the World". That was the begin-

ning of numerous enjoyable quilting experiences that we have had together. From there, I became the "Trip Queen".

At a quilt show, I bought my one and only purchased quilt which was a "Trip Around the World" by Dawn at Cherrywood Fabrics. It was very inspiring and still hangs in our Florida home. From then on, I made dozens of "Trips"; King-size, Queen-size, Twin-size, Baby-size --- whatever the occasion, births, birthdays, weddings, graduations, holidays, anniversaries, etc., I made a quilt for it. Check out our book "Sulky Secrets to Successful Quilting" #900B-13 for how-to instructions to make easy "Trip Around the World" quilts.

When we were not traveling doing trade shows or other appearances, a group of

friends would meet at our retail store and sew on Sundays when the shop was closed. We would share stories about what went on all week and what we found that was new with sewing, etc. It was our much-needed special time together as friends.

And when we started Sulky of America in 1987 and I began to tape TV shows for PBS in Milwaukee, WI, it only seemed natural for Patti and I to stay over the weekend and take a quilting class at a favorite shop we found there. For years we did this and we branched out to make all sorts of quilts. We called our group the "Half-Wits" since we got together twice a year.

I had this dream that I would make a Postage Stamp Quilt like Georgia Bonesteel's, using over 5,000 different fabrics. Of course, with this quilt in mind we had to frequent every fabric store we saw, and our fabric stashes grew.

Fred said we were insulating our home with fabric for this one quilt! While the quilt has yet to be completed, after 30 years of collecting, we do have the fabric stash for it and more!

Well, all things change and so did our quilting. My friend Carol Ingram and I started designing computer embroidery designs for Cactus Punch and Amazing Designs and, of course, we began featuring these designs on our quilts which we would show on some of the PBS-TV shows when we were guests.

When the studio in WI closed and we started taping in Cleveland, OH, our good friend, Sue Hausmann, knew we had given up a weekend quilting group and we were grieving the loss, so she introduced us to Nancy and Bev at Abigayle's Quiltery in Olmsted Falls, OH.

We didn't think we could ever have it as good as we did with our friends in Milwaukee, but we soon learned that we had really found a home with Bev and Nancy at Abigayle's. Since we started taping shows in Cleveland four times a year, we got to have four quilting weekends with them to look forward to throughout the year. We think we all must have been meant to meet because Bev and Nancy have become as close as sisters to Patti, Carol and I.

Because of this connection, and their tremendous creativity, they have contributed greatly to this book. They have been teaching people to quilt by hand and machine since 1999 and have

inspired so many more with the quilt patterns they have written.

And the weekend quilting with friends continues in the Smoky Mountains of NC where Carol, Patti, Sharon Stokes, Nancy Sapin and I are neighbors. We all get together on the weekends whenever we can and quilt fun projects to share with all of you.

A special thanks to our other contributors as well ---Pam Damour of Pam Damour Designs, Pam Laba from Port Charlotte, FL, Nancy Sapin from Franklin, NC, Sue Moats from Silver Springs, MD and expert designer and long-arm quilter extraordiniare, Evelyn Byler, from Topeka, IN.

Also thank you to our editors: Fred Drexler and Patti Lee and our photographers, Claudia Lopez and Chuck Humbert.

Contact your local PBS station for the days and times that they air the shows that I appear on: "America Sews with Sue Hausmann", "America Quilts Creatively", and "Fons & Porter".

--- Joyce Drexler

Start quilting this weekend and enjoy the company of friends!

Nancy Bryant

Co-owner of Abigayle's Quiltery in Cleveland, OH. She has sewn her entire life, starting in fashion and moving to quilting. She designs, sews, and teaches almost every waking hour of the day. Nancy is a Pfaff Certified Teacher.

Beverly Morris

Co-owner of Abigayle's Quiltery in Cleveland, OH. She has been a sewing fanatic her entire life. When she discovered quilting, she became completely enthralled. She is a pattern designer as well as a Pfaff Certified Teacher.

Carol Ingram

Carol's 45 years of sewing experience provides her with special insight into combining art and textiles. She is a "Sewing Star", author and designer for Sulky of America, as well as a designer for Cactus Punch and others.

Patti Lee

Patti is V.P. of Consumer Relations for Sulky. She has over 30 years experience in the sewing industry and she has contributed to many of the Sulky books.

2

General Supplies

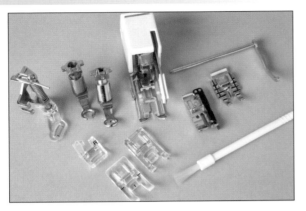

- Zig-Zag Sewing Machine that you love - cleaned and tuned up
- *Optional:* Embroidery machine and/or Embroidery Unit, Hoops and Embroidery Design Cards
- 1/4" Foot and Walking Foot (possibly NOT included with a basic zig-zag sewing machine)
- Free-Motion Darning/Quilting Foot
- Open-Toe Applique Foot
- Edge Foot • Cording Foot
- Stitch-in-the-Ditch Foot
- Large Cutting Mat

- Quilter's Acrylic Rulers - 6-1/2" x 24", 12-1/2" x 24", 6" and 12" square (from Brandy's™)
- The Triangle™ Ruler by Little Foot™
- Masking Tape or Binder Clips
- Quilting Pins and Pin Cushion
- Clover™ Chalk Markers • Water Soluble Pen
- Seam Ripper • Large and Small Scissors
- Machine Needles: *See Thread Chart page 16.*
    for Piecing - 12/80 Universal
    for Quilting - 14/90 and 16/100
    for Metallic Thread - 14/90
    for Embroidery - 12/80 or 14/90, 16/100
- Free-Motion Quilting/Embroidery Hoops
- 2" Finished Half-Square Triangle Paper
- Steam Iron with non-stick sole plate
- 1/4" Steam-A-Seam™ on the roll.
- Hand Quilting Supplies on page 35.

Color Coded Sulky Stabilizers - for Quilting:

Water Soluble - Solvy™, Super Solvy™, Ultra Solvy™, Paper Solvy™, and Fabri-Solvy™

Tear-Aways - Tear-Easy™, Stiffy™, and Totally Stable™

Cut-Aways - Soft 'n Sheer™ and Fuse 'n Stitch™
Sulky KK 2000™ Temporary Spray Adhesive

Sulky Threads:

- Sulky 12 wt. & 30 wt. solid color Cotton Thread
- Sulky 12 wt. & 30 wt. Cotton Blendables™
- Sulky 40 wt. and 30 wt. Rayon Thread
- Sulky Holoshimmer™ Metallic Thread
- Sulky Sliver™ Metallic Thread
- Sulky Bobbin Thread
- Sulky Invisible Thread

Fabric Selection

A beautiful handmade quilt can last a lifetime if it is made with good quality 100% cotton fabrics. Thread count, fabric dyes, finishes, and design come together to make a fine fabric. Some of our favorite fabric manufacturers are Hoffman, Robert Kaufman, Michael Miller, Timeless Treasures, Moda, RJR, P&B, Maywood Studio, VIP, Clothworks, In The Beginning, Benartex, Chanteclaire, Lake House, Alexander Henry, Windham Fabrics and Free-Spirit, to name just a few, with new companies on the horizon.

Quality, high-thread-count fabrics are easier to work with and they produce superior results. As you progress in your quilting endeavors, take note of the manufacturers that produce the most pleasing, enduring results for you.

Pre-wash the fabric in a gentle quilt soap such as Orvis Paste™ to pre-shrink it and remove any excess dyes. Separate the darks from the lights to assure color integrity.

Cotton fabrics are generally found in 44-45" widths. After pre-washing, remove selvages; 40–42" of fabric will be usable. Consider this when estimating fabric requirements. It is always a good idea to buy a little extra to be sure.

The fabric amounts suggested in the projects have built-in extra amounts for those unexpected oh-no's!

Fabric Tips:

1. Clip the corners of your fabric yardage before washing to prevent excess raveling. This will also help you to know that this fabric has been washed when you take it from your stash in the future.
2. Use a Dye Magnet™ in the wash cycle to draw loose dyes from the wash water.
3. For maximum pre-shrinkage, remove fabric from the dryer while it is still damp, and iron it dry.
4. Always keep your eyes open for great stash builders. Quilters collect fabric and need to build a color palette. Fabric designs are printed in limited quantities. If you like it, buy it when you see it!
5. Use Sulky Soft 'n Sheer™ on the backside of a block to line it, to prevent show-through, and to stabilize light-colored or sheer fabrics.

Rotary Cutting

The quilt designs in this book are designed for strip-pieced, rotary cutting techniques. Speed, accuracy and ease of use are benefits of the rotary cutter which was invented in the 1970's. Before that, quilters had to make templates and cut each piece separately with scissors. Today, we can accurately cut multiple pieces with one, single, time-saving pass of the cutter.

Once the fabric is washed and pressed, gently refold the fabric along the manufacturer's fold line. Use the acrylic ruler to line up the marks on the ruler with the fold line. If this is done carefully, it will produce a perfect 90° edge.

Read the cutting instructions that came with your rotary cutter. Be very careful with the blade because it is as sharp as a surgical knife. **EVERY TIME THE CUTTER IS PUT DOWN, BE SURE IT IS CLOSED AND, PREFERABLY, LOCKED.**

To prepare to cut, place your hand on the ruler and press it firmly against the fabric. Hold the cutter and align the blade of the cutter with the edge of the ruler. Using a continuously firm downward pressure, always push the cutter away from your body. Start by trimming away the uneven edge from one edge of the fabric. Now there is a starting place for measuring perfectly sized strips. Use the marks on the ruler to measure the strip size indicated on the pattern.

Cutting Tips:

1. *To maintain accuracy, re-straighten the edge of the fabric after every three or four cuts. In general, the fabric will be accurate only to the width of the ruler used to straighten the edge. After that width, the fabric may angle slightly and cause the fabric strip to "dogleg" when unfolded.*

2. *Try a new ergonomic cutter that automatically closes when it is dropped or laid down.*

3. *Many products are available to keep the acrylic ruler from slipping on the fabric. Choose a product that does not raise the level of the ruler which could enable the cutter to angle and change the size of the cut fabric strip. We highly recommend InvisiGRIP by Omnigrid which will cover the backs of several rulers.*

4. *Another method to keep the ruler from slipping is to place the hand that holds the ruler slightly off the far edge while holding it firmly against the fabric. This is a good method for people with hand or joint difficulties.*

5. *Some people prefer to use the "walking method" of holding the ruler. While cutting, hold the ruler straight down with the pads of the fingers. When about halfway done with the cut, stop and carefully lift the holding hand, "walk" the fingers toward the other end of the ruler and press straight down firmly. Finish the cut.*

6. *Try cutting multiple strips with one pass. The 60mm rotary cutter is a must. It will not distort the fabric while cutting cleanly through eight layers of fabric. Layer the fabrics, aligning the folds to be perfectly parallel. Remember that every time a fabric is layered for cutting, precious time for sewing has been saved, sometimes reducing the needed cutting time by more than half!*

7. *Just like a razor, rotary blades dull and often get nicks. Sharpening can be done with a rotary cutter sharpening stone or by a professional scissor sharpening business. Replace blades when needed.*

Piecing Tips

Sewing machine companies are taking very good care of quilting customers by making available specialty feet for virtually any machine. Quilters require a perfect quarter-inch seam. Often this is best achieved with a quarter-inch foot. Some machines can move the needle position to get the right size seam. Still others may need a mark on the needle plate. To make sure you are getting an accurate quarter-inch seam, sew three 1-1/2" wide strips together lengthwise. Press the seams toward the outside strips. Does the center strip measure exactly 1" wide?

"Chain piecing" is another quilting technique that can save time when sewing similar pieces. Immediately after sewing two pieces together, insert another set into the sewing machine. Don't clip threads. Allow them to stay "chained" together until you have pressed carefully, then clip the chain apart.

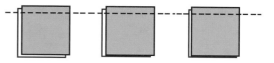

1"

When quilts are put together with many, many seams, a very small inaccuracy in each seam can add up to an amazingly wrong-sized quilt top! Take the time to check the accuracy of your quarter-inch seams now.

When piecing fabrics for a quilt, place fabrics right sides together. Sew, using a quarter-inch seam and ten to twelve stitches per inch. Backtacking at the beginning and end of seams is not necessary except in some advanced quilt patterns. Each seam is generally crossed by another seam, therefore there is no stress at the ends of the seam.

Piecing Tips:

1. *If the seams pucker and refuse to lie flat, rethread the machine and check the thread tension and needle size. If this does not correct the problem, stabilize it by placing strips of Sulky lightweight Tear-Easy under the seam during sewing. Simply tear it away before pressing.*

2. *Sewing machines that have the "needle stop down" feature are a great investment. When the needle stops in the down position, the fabric is held in place, the tension is maintained, and chain piecing is streamlined. The ability to pivot with the needle down is an even greater asset when quilting or appliquéing.*

3. *The best investment in quilting is the quarter-inch foot! Look for a quality foot with side markings, or a foot with a side bar. Ask a machine dealer for a foot that is made specifically for your sewing machine; if unavailable, check out Little Foot™, a manufacturer of generic, specialty feet. (Contact them at www.littlefoot.com.)*

Pressing Tips

In quilt making, the seams are pressed together toward one side, unlike garment making where they are pressed open. The closed seams provide strength to the finished quilt.

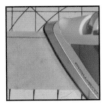 With an iron set on cotton, press the seams as sewn. First, press the seam flat (this sets the seam), then press the seam to one side (usually 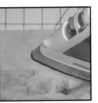 toward the darker fabric) by setting the iron directly down firmly on the fabric, then lifting straight up. Do not slide the iron back and forth because that can distort the fabric strips.

As a general rule, seams are usually pressed either toward the darker of the two fabrics or away from the bulk. To use or not use steam is a hot topic among quilters. Beginners may distort the shape of the patchwork squares or shrink the fabric by using steam.

Embroidery and appliqué should always be pressed on a soft surface from the wrong side of the fabric.

Irons come in all sizes and types, and with many different features. Although the automatic shut-off is a wonderful safety feature, many quilters find it inconvenient. Also, consider purchasing one of the miniature irons to set beside your sewing machine or to take to a class. For home use, consider a lightweight iron with a pointed end.

In this book, you will find arrows with the graphics indicating which way seams should be pressed.

Pressing Tips:

1. Pay attention to the pressing instructions in the quilt pattern. They will help make the block lay flat and reduce the bulk to make quilting easier.
2. Spray starch is an organic product used to stiffen fabric. Sizing performs the same function, but it is a man-made product. Some quilters use these products to give a professional finish to a block.
3. Use a press cloth to prevent fabric from scorching or seam imprinting.
4. Portable pressing pads save space and can be set up right next to the sewing machine. Some pressing pads have a cutting mat on the other side.

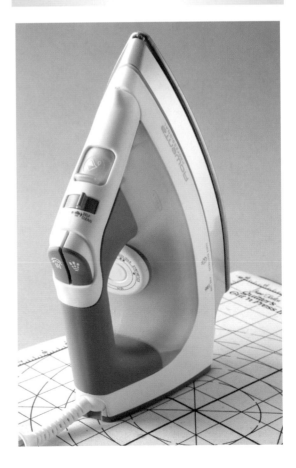

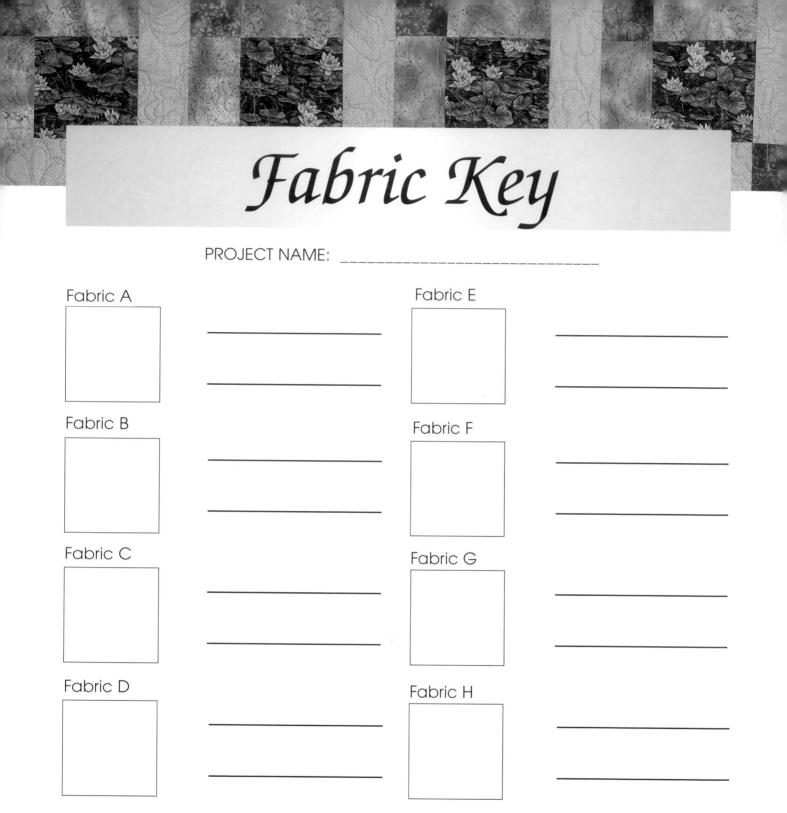

Fabric Key

PROJECT NAME: _____

Fabric A

_____

_____

Fabric B

_____

_____

Fabric C

_____

_____

Fabric D

_____

_____

Fabric E

_____

_____

Fabric F

_____

_____

Fabric G

_____

_____

Fabric H

_____

_____

How to use a Fabric Key:

Before starting a project, set up a Fabric Key with a small sample of the actual fabrics to be used in the project. When using different colored fabrics than what the book sample shows, a Fabric Key is essential to keep you from making costly mistakes. Paste a 1" sample of the fabric in the box, then write a brief description of where to use it on the lines next to the box. If more than 8 fabrics are used, photocopy an extra sheet, cross through the printed letter, and put additional letters as needed.

Making Triangles

Option 1 - Make 2" Finished Half-Square Triangles using 2 Fabrics and Triangle Paper Sheets or Triangles on a Roll.

1. Cut two 10" x 16" pieces of fabric, 1 light and 1 dark. Lightly spray Sulky KK 2000 onto the right side of the dark piece and place the light piece on top of it, with right sides together. Lightly spray KK 2000 onto the wrong side of the top fabric and place the sheet of half-square triangle paper on top of it, right side up. You now have a nice "sandwich" that will stay together without pinning while you sew.

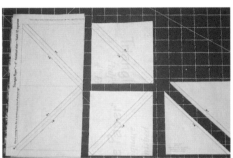

2. Insert a size 90/14 topstitch needle. To make the triangle paper tear away more easily, use Sulky 30 wt. Cotton Thread in both the top and the bobbin, and straight stitch on the dotted lines with a short stitch length (2.0). Use your ruler and rotary cutter to cut the half-squares apart on the solid lines.

3. Press the seam toward the dark fabric. While supporting the stitching line, gently tear off the triangle paper.

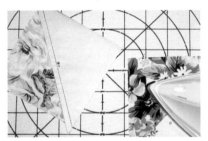

Note: A way to remember which fabric should be on the bottom is ... "DD" Dark side down. One sheet of 2" finished triangle paper (prepared as noted) will yield 30 half-square triangles.

Triangle Tips:

1. To help stabilize any fabrics that may want to be "contrary", leave the paper on the triangles until the back is pieced.
2. To free the paper from the stitching, gently pull the block diagonally along the seam lines.
3. Make up your own triangles on Sulky Paper Solvy. Using your drawing, and Paper Solvy, run off sheets using a copier. Once stitched in a project there is no need to tear-away the paper, just submerge in warm water and the Paper Solvy dissolves away. Let dry. Press.

Option 2 - For a "scrappy look", make 2" Finished Half-Square Triangles from a variety of colors of 3" Fabric Squares.

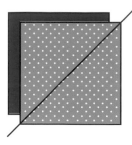 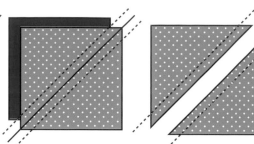 

1. Draw or press a diagonal line from corner to corner on the wrong side of (2) 3" light squares.

May we suggest: . . .

Right after Step 2, try using the Quilt-in-a-Day™ Triangle Square-Up Ruler. It will halve the trim time.

2. Since these squares will be sewn on the bias, to minimize shifting and stretching, lightly spray the right sides of the light squares with Sulky KK-2000 Temporary Spray Adhesive and layer these light squares with the 3" dark squares, right sides together. Sew a scant 1/4" away from both sides of the drawn line. Cut apart on the drawn line.

3. Open and press seams to the dark side. Trim these half-square triangles to 2" by lining up on the 45° mark on your ruler.

Making Setting Triangles - Using The Triangle Tool™

To cut setting triangles:

1. Once you have pieced all your blocks, measure them to find the unfinished block size. If blocks are not the same size, use the largest one.

2. On your Setting Triangle, find your unfinished block size down the side of the triangle tool.

3. Follow the solid black line to the center of the triangle.

4. Cut one strip of fabric

the size indicated in the middle of the Setting Triangle tool.

5. Place the tool on the strip of fabric and align the bottom edge of your fabric with the correct line that corresponds to your unfinished block size.

6. Hold the tool securely with one hand and, with the other hand, firmly cut along both edges of the Setting Triangle tool.

7. Now, grab the bottom of your Setting Triangle tool and flip it up and out so that you are now looking at the Setting Triangle tool upside down.

8. Align the TOP of your fabric with the same previous line. Cut down one side of the Setting Triangle.

9. Cut triangles from entire strip. See how many Setting Triangles you can get from one strip, and cut more strips accordingly.

Making Corner Triangles Using The Triangle Tool™

To cut corner triangles:

1. Find the size of your unfinished block down the side.

2. Move one line up. (For example, if your unfinished block is 6 inches, you would use the 6-1/2" line.) Follow the line across to determine the width of your strip.

3. Cut a strip to this size. Using the same directions as above, cut two triangles from your fabric. Once again, use the appropriate line as a guide.

4. To make 4 corner triangles, slice these two triangles in half from the top 90° angle to the base or longest side of the triangle. The outside edges are on the straight grain to minimize stretch.

5. Add each triangle to the four corners of your quilt top. Press the quilt top carefully, then align your long ruler along the edge with the 1/4 inch line along the intersections. Square up your quilt. A little "fudge factor" has been allowed to accommodate the difference in each individual's sewing habit.

Printed with permission from Lynn Graves, Little Foot Ltd.
See Sources page 177.

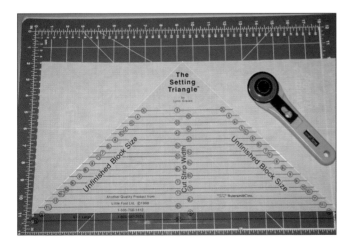

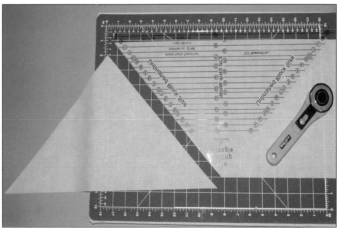

Stabilizers for Quilters

What are stabilizers?

To those who have used stabilizers, they are the magic cure-all! They make the end result of our creative machine work look professionally done.

But why would a quilter or home decorator need stabilizers?

Today's quilter wants to do more than just seam pieces of cloth together and stitch in the ditch to quilt; they want to go further and apply a quilting design or embellish their quilt top.

We use "topper" stabilizers as a template which allows us to have a quilting design to follow without marking directly on the quilt, risking the possible reappearance of markings.

We use "backing" stabilizers to relieve the stress placed on the fabric being embellished; they reduce or eliminate puckering, tunneling, or other unwanted reactions. Some can be used as the foundation on which our creative machine work is done.

We can also use stabilizers as templates for cutting, and for turning appliques.

Read on to understand when and where to use different stabilizers for the best results.

Sulky Water Soluble Solvys

Stiffen Fabric for Embellishing:
The apple border above is featured in a quilt on page 87. Before piecing the quilt, the apple fabric was immersed in a solution of Sulky Solvy and water to stiffen the fabric, which made it easier to add free-motion embroidery. Four of the Sulky Solvys (Solvy, Super Solvy, Ultra Solvy or Fabri-Solvy) can be dissolved and used this way.

For example: put a 20" x 36" piece of Solvy (the lightest density) in 8 oz. of warm water; let the Solvy dissolve, then submerge the fabric in it. Remove the fabric (do not rinse) and allow it to dry. Iron the fabric to remove any wrinkles before embellishing. Store the unused portion in the refrigerator in a labeled jar that is tightly sealed.

Once the embellishing is accomplished, rinse the fabric thoroughly to remove the stabilizer. This method is ideal when embellishing flimsy fabrics like rayon or bridal fabrics that can be laundered.

Use Sulky Solvy to make your own unique fabric: Trap yarns and/or snippets of thread and fabric between two layers of Sulky Solvy. Stick it all together with a quick press of a dry iron that has a non-stick sole plate. Stitch over it with Sulky threads to keep it all together. Rinse away the Solvy, let dry, press flat and you have fabric!

Use Paper Solvy instead of Triangle Paper or Foundation Piecing paper:
No more tearing away the paper, it will just dissolve away the first time the quilt is laundered!

Use Solvy to turn Appliques:
Lightly spray Sulky KK 2000 onto Solvy and smooth it onto the right side of the applique piece; straight stitch around it using a scant 1/4". Slit the Solvy and turn it to the back, which turns under the seam allowance. Press with a warm, dry iron. No more endless hours of needle-turning appliques.

Use Fabri-Solvy as a quilt design template:
No more need for messy chalk markers or air or water soluble markers that may come back to haunt you, or the time-consuming tearing away of paper! Just draw the design on Fabri-Solvy, lightly spritz the fabric with water, and smooth the Solvy Quilt Pattern over the fabric.

Let dry, then stitch over the design. To remove the Fabri-Solvy, simply launder the quilt when all the quilting is done. Fill your top loading washer with warm water only - NO SOAP. Allow the washer to agitate the quilt for 3-5 minutes to remove the Solvy. Then, add mild soap to launder as desired. This way your quilt is clean and sweet-smelling when you get ready to use it or give it away!

13

Use a Solvy Stabilizer as a foundation for creating fringe -
See the pillows featured on pages 84 and 85.

Use Ultra Solvy Stabilizer as a foundation for creating computer or free-motion lace embellishments for quilted projects -
This strong, water soluble stabilizer will withstand the repeated needle penetrations that occur when making lace on the sewing machine.

Nationally known teacher, Jim Suzio, suggests using Sulky Solvy to eliminate hoop burn...

"When doing free-motion, computerized or hand embroidery or quilting, Solvy will eliminate the damage to fabric caused by the friction of the inner hoop being inserted into the outer hoop; plus the transparent Solvy allows you to easily see your placement marks. When you dissolve it, no bulk is added to your embroidery, and the fabric remains unmarked."

For even more ideas and tips, refer to the book: *Sulky Secrets to Successful Stabilizing.*

Sulky Tear-away Stabilizers

Use Sulky Tear Easy or Totally Stable when doing buttonhole or blanket, machine-stitched appliques.

Even if the fabric being stitched is stable, Tear-Easy or Totally Stable will still help your sewing machine create more even and accurate decorative stitches on the applique.

Try ironing Totally Stable onto the back of fabric prior to fusing on an iron-on applique. This helps eliminate shifting and stretching during fusing and allows for beautiful buttonhole stitching around the fused fabric applique. It is a breeze to remove. Always support the stitching with your fingers while tearing away one layer at a time.

Nationally known quilter and author, Katie Pasquini suggests using Sulky Totally Stable for turned edge piecing . . . *"I have been quilting for 25 years, but I had a difficult time working out techniques using tracing paper as a foundation. I have been using Totally Stable, iron-on, tear-away stabilizer for over 15 years and I love it. It holds my turned edge stable and my piece is really flat and ready to quilt."*

Nationally known designer, quilter, and author, Virginia Avery says . . .
"Most of my machine quilting is done through two layers only (the shell, or out-side layer, and the batting); Tear-Easy is perfect for this, as it protects the feed dogs from the batting. Since I work with wearables almost exclusively, and work with a mix of fabrics, it's great to know there is a Sulky stabilizer that can take care of any situation in stitching."

Nationally known quilter, author, and TV personality, Sharlene Jorgenson uses Sulky Tear-Easy Stabilizer as a foundation support for crazy patchwork by machine . . .
"I find it to be the best stabilizer for Crazy Patchwork by machine since it supports the decorative stitching no matter whether it is stitched in Sulky Rayon or Sulky Metallic Thread, and it does not tear out the delicate stitching when removed."

14

Sulky Cut-Away Stabilizers

Jeanie Sexton, award winning free-motion expert says . . *Sulky permanent Cut-Away Soft 'n Sheer is a wonderful foundation for free-motion embroidery and computerized stitching because it is strong enough to hold the built-up threads, yet pliable enough to be an excellent base. It can be used alone so there will be a more delicate, finished motif."*

Sulky Soft 'n Sheer works as the perfect lining to block out shine-through on sheer or lightweight fabrics.

See the Placemat Project on page 83.

Sulky Soft 'n Sheer is used to make 3-D computer embroideries for quilted projects.

Soft 'n Sheer is soft, yet it will support the load of stitches in computer embroidery without adding stiffness. It trims away cleanly from the stitched edge and can even be burned away with a wood burning tool because of its nylon consistency.

Sulky Cut-Away Plus or Sulky Fuse 'n Stitch make the perfect inner lining for totes or quilted bags.

Using two layers of Cut-Away Plus or ironing one to two layers of Sulky Fuse 'n Stitch permanent stabilizer will give extra body and support to cotton fabrics, causing your quilted tote or bag to stand up tall without adding stiffness.

See the Knitting Bag Project on page 94.

What is KK 2000™ Temporary Spray Adhesive?

- Non-Toxic
- Odorless
- Drys Clear
- Air Soluble
- Concentrated
- Non-Flammable
- Ozone Friendly
- No CFC's or HCFC's
- Heavier than air Propellent.

How would you use KK 2000 Temporary Spray Adhesive?

- Spray KK 2000 in short bursts at a distance of 6" to 10", onto one surface only. Finger-press that surface onto the receiving surface, and you can stitch immediately without gumming up the needle.

- Spray any of the Sulky Stabilizers (except Ultra Solvy and Heat-Away) to make them a self-stick stabilizer to embroider difficult-to-hoop items like pockets, edges, button rows, ribbons, cuffs, collars, socks, neckties, handkerchiefs, doll clothes, etc. Spray on paper patterns or stencils for easy tracing and cutting.

- One short spray of KK 2000 is usually sufficent, while highly flammable, lighter-than-air, butane-propelled adhesives usually need the equivalent of 2 or more cloud-producing sprays that can float out into the room.

- Spray the back of quilt tops and backings when layering quilts with fleece or batting.

- Spray the back of appliques to make them repositionable when designing.

- Spray fabric to fabric, and then spray triangle paper to avoid using pins.

15

A Beginner's Quick Reference Guide to using Sulky® Threads for Machine-Fed or Free-Motion Quilting

Type of Sulky Thread	Solid Colors available	Variegated Colors available	Multi-Colors available	Type and Size Needle to use	Spool Pin vertical	Spool Pin horizontal	Top Tension	Can be used in Bobbin	Yardage on Regular Spool	Yardage on King Size Spool	Yardage on Jumbo Cones	Machine Washable, Dryable, and Dry Cleanable
30 wt. Rayon	102	36	18	Embroidery/ Top Stitch 90 or 100	ok	ok	Loosen Slightly	yes	180	500	5,500	* yes
40 wt. Rayon	333	36	19	Embroidery 80 or 90	ok	ok	Loosen Slightly	yes	250	850	5,500	* yes
40 wt. Poly Deco	138	0	0	Embroidery 75 or 90	ok	ok	Loosen Slightly	ok	250	900	5,500	* yes
Original Metallic	27	0	9	Metallic or Topstitch 14/90	ok	ok	Loosen Slightly	yes with care	165	1,000	N/A	yes
Sliver Metallic	22	0	2	Metallic or Topstitch 14/90	must	no	Loosen a lot	yes with care	250	N/A	N/A	* yes
Holoshimmer	22	0	2	Metallic or Topstitch 14/90	must	no	Very Loose	yes with care	250	N/A	N/A	* yes
12 wt. Cotton/Blendables	66	0	84	Denim or Topstitch 90 or 100	no	ok	Very Loose	yes	N/A	330	2,100	* yes
30 wt. Cotton/Blendables	66	0	84	Denim or Topstitch 14/90	no	ok	Loosen Slightly	yes	N/A	500	3,200	* yes
Polyester Invisible	2	0	0	Embroidery 75 or 90	no	ok	Loosen Slightly	yes wind slowly	440	2,200	N/A	* yes
Polyester Bobbin	2	0	0	N/A	ok	ok	N/A	yes	475	1,100	N/A	yes

Attributes of each type of Sulky Thread and what they are mostly used for.

All are made from the highest quality raw goods available in the world, and they all come on snap-end spools that allow you to store your thread ends neatly. Ease the snap-end open gently with your thumb.

* Indicates that it is color-fast when washed with detergents that do not contain chlorine or optical brighteners.

✓Very much the same luster as silk with silk's smoothness, but it is stronger than both silk and cotton thread. ✓Won't fray, fuzz or shrink. ✓Less stretch than Polyester Thread. ✓Perfect for all machine work, sergers, knitting machines and handwork. ✓White can be over-dyed. Sulky 40 wt. Rayon is the thread most digitizers of computerized embroidery designs use as a standard. Sulky 30 wt. Rayon is 1/3 heavier than 40 wt. and 2/3 heavier than 50 wt. for greater visibility, depth and unique color interest in decorative stitching and quilting. Industry experts calculate that one 250 yd. Sulky 40 wt. Rayon spool can create 44,000 embroidery stitches, while an 850 yd. Sulky king-size spool can create 156,000 stitches, and a 1,500 yd. spool can create 273,000 stitches. Also available in all colors on Jumbo Cones.

✓It is extremely strong and can also be used for general seam sewing. ✓It is color-fast when washed with detergents that contain chlorine or optical brighteners which makes it ideal for embroidery on children's clothes, sports clothes and uniforms. ✓Has a more "plastic" luster than rayon.

✓It is a round, twisted thread of metallic fibers over a strong core. ✓It does not fuzz, fray or shrink. ✓Since all Metallics hate abrasion, always use a 14/90 needle, soft pliable stabilizer, and a lightweight bobbin thread; sew slower. ✓Dry at low heat. ✓Drycleanable.

✓Both are a thin, flat, ribbon-like polyester film that is metalized with an aluminum layer to give it a brilliant reflectiveness. ✓Holoshimmer is made with a holographic layer and is somewhat stronger than Sliver. ✓Does not fuzz, fray or shrink. ✓Use only on a **vertical spool pin** since it is a flat thread; the twisting action from unwinding off a horizontal spool pin can cause breakage. ✓When winding onto a bobbin, use a slow speed only. ✓Always use a 14/90 needle, soft pliable stabilizer, and a lightweight bobbin thread; sew slower. ✓Dry at low heat settings. Drycleanable. Do not apply direct heat from an iron.

✓2-ply 100% premium long staple Egyptian Cotton. ✓Matte finish. Solids are perfect to make a country, primitive or antique look. ✓It does fuzz and will shrink slightly. ✓Very soft feel. ✓White can be dyed. ✓Hand embroiderers and quilters find it the perfect weight and texture and prefer it over floss since it comes on a convenient spool that will not tangle. ✓All 84 Blendables are multi-colors; 56 of them are subtle and masterful blends of different colors within the same range of tone and intensity. ✓Randomly change color every 2-1/2" to 5". ✓Perfect for today's mottled or batik dyed fabrics. ✓28 Blendables are primary including red, white and blue and black and white! They were designed by Joyce Drexler to blend with current fabric lines. They are available on King Spools and Jumbo Cones in all colors.

✓It is a very fine .004 cross-wound monofilament of 100% Polyester. ✓Softer, more flexible and more heat tolerant than nylon. ✓It comes in Smoke and Clear on small or king-size snap-end spools. ✓Wind on bobbin slowly. ✓It does not fuzz, fray or shrink.

✓Lightweight (60 wt.) spun polyester. ✓Commonly used in the bobbin for digitized computer embroidery. ✓Won't fray, fuzz or shrink. ✓Available in both black and white on small and king-size snap-end spools.

Sulky Slimline Boxes

You can purchase Sulky Threads in a variety of prepackaged assortments in Slimline Storage Boxes, or purchase the boxes empty.

Visit www.sulky.com to view all of the available assortments, including Blendables Dream Packages. Sulky's "No-spill" Slimline and Universal Storage Boxes are made of a durable plastic and weigh under 5 pounds when full. They are ideal for lint-free storage at home or for taking your threads to classes and retreats. Free labels are available to sort your threads by color number or color family.

Sulky Slimline Assortments are available for all the different types of Sulky Thread includ-ing:

- 12 & 30 wt. Cotton Blendables
- 12 & 30 wt. Solid Color Cottons
- 40 wt. & 30 wt. Rayons
- 40 wt. Poly Deco
- Sulky Metallics

Fabric Bowl Project found on page 135

Sulky Blendables™

Sulky Blendables™

New! Sulky's 84 Multi-color Blendables™ Cotton Thread

Sulky Blendables range from subtle to bold. These magnificent multi-color cotton threads from Sulky randomly change color every couple of inches. Just think of the colorful quilts, appliques and embroideries you will create with this one-of-a-kind, 100% Egyptian Cotton, highly mercerized, long staple thread. Sulky Blendables are a masterful blend of different colors within the same range of tone and intensity, and a dream to quilt with.

Blendables were developed by Joyce Drexler to coordinate with many manufacturer's fabric lines like Thimbleberries™. (Used on the bowl pictured on the left.)

■ Two Weights:

30 wt. (2/3 thicker than 50 wt.) is ideal in the bobbin and through a size 14/90 machine quilting or topstitch needle. 30 wt. comes on both 500 yd. snap-end King spools and 3,300 yd. snap-end Jumbo Cones. Snap-ends are terrific because you can gently snap them open and closed to release thread ends or neatly store them.

12 wt. is even heavier (40% thicker than 30 wt.) and therefore adds more texture to your quilting. It is best used through a size 14/90 or 16/100 topstitch needle. 12 wt. comes on both 330 yd. snap-end King spools and 2,100 yd. snap-end Jumbo Cones. We love to use 12 wt. on the top of the quilt and a matching 30 wt. in the bobbin for great results on both sides of a quilt.

Both weights are now available in 84 fantastic, mouth-watering multi-colors.

They blend beautifully when you quilt batiks, mottled solids, florals or any multi-colored or shaded fabric. One "Blendable" will work with many different colored and printed fabrics. The blending effects that you can create with these heavier 100% Cotton Threads are like nothing you have ever seen, and they are absolutely stunning on solid color fabrics. Also, look for Blendables in filled Sulky *Universal Slimline Storage Box Assortments. A must-have for any quilter or sewer.*

■ Great for Crafts

Blendables are also used in all types of sewing, serging and hand crafts. Great for Punchneedle because they are a continuous filament that doesn't tangle like floss and needs no constant rethreading of the needle like floss does. A real time-saver!

Punchneedle using
Sulky Cotton Thread.
By Pearl Periera
of P3 Designs.
www.P3Designs.com

Kids love using them to make friendship bracelets. Great for blanket-stitching with wools and for a new interesting look for outline embroideries.

Sulky Solid Cottons

Sulky's 66 Solid Colors of 12 wt. and 30 wt., Highly Mercerized, Premium Long-fiber, 100% Egyptian Cotton Thread for quilting and more!

Because all Sulky Cotton Thread is made from the highest quality, highly mercerized Egyptian Cotton available in the world, there are no problems with thread breaking, unraveling or deteriorating as a result of poor quality thread. Years of engineering and research have gone into perfecting the performance of today's Sulky Cotton Decorative Thread. From raw goods to twisting, and from dyeing to finishing, all ingredients of thread manufacturing are combined perfectly to produce the smoothest Sulky Cotton Thread that is still strong enough to survive today's machine evolution.

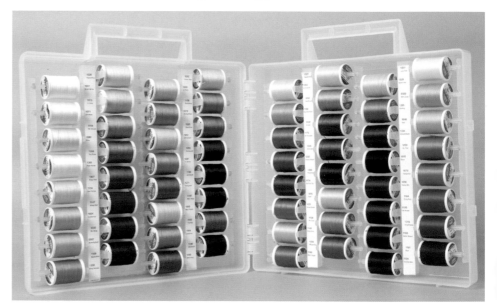

Both weights are available in 66 fabulous solid colors that are ideal wherever a matte finish is desired. You can buy 64 of either weight in a filled Sulky Universal Slimline Storage Box Assortment. Perfect for Hand and Machine Quilting.

Visit: www.sulky.com to see more assortments.

30 wt. Cotton

30 wt. is ideal in the bobbin and on top through a size 14/90 machine quilting or topstitch needle. All 30 wt. comes on both a 500 yd. snap-end King spool and on a 3,300 yd. snap-end Jumbo Cone. It is the perfect piecing thread. See pages 51, 65, 112, 113, and 117 for computer embroidery designs using Sulky 30 wt. Cotton.

12 wt. Cotton

12 wt. is heavier which adds more texture to your quilting. It is best used through a size 14/90 or 16/100 topstitch needle, and all 12 wt. comes on both a 330 yd. snap-end King spool and a 2,100 yd. snap-end Jumbo Cone. For great results on both sides of the quilt, we like to feature 12 wt. on the top and a matching 30 wt. in the bobbin. Because one strand of 12 wt. is equal to 2 strands of embroidery floss, it is a very versatile thread that is perfect for hand crafts like crochet, punchneedle, cross stitch, and embroidery; and it is great for sewing machine and serger techniques like couching, applique, bobbin work, and quilting.

Sulky 30 wt. Rayons

30 wt. Rayon

30 wt. is the heavier Rayon Thread that is ideal for quilting when a more reflective sheen is desired than Sulky Cotton has.

It is 1/3 thicker than 40 wt. Rayon and 2/3 thicker than 50 wt. thread for greater visibility, depth, and unique color interest in quilting and applique stitches.

Sulky 30 wt. Rayon Thread is available in 156 luscious colors; 102 solid and 54 variegated and multi-colors on a 180 yd. snap-end spool, a 500 yd. snap-end King spool, and a 5,500 yd. snap-end Jumbo Cone in virtually all colors.

With Sulky's snap-end spools...

- *No more thread falling off the spool and tangling under the spool pin.*
- *No more unprotected, exposed thread at the end of the spool or cone that can become trapped by the spool holder.*
- *No more need to use thread nets.*
- *No more tangled messes in your thread storage boxes.*
- *No more spools or cones that don't turn smoothly and evenly on vertical spool pins.*
- *No more sticky, gooey labels that make it difficult to get the thread out from under.*

30 wt. Rayon Spools have Red print on small spools.

Fabric Bowl Project found on page 135.

Sulky 40 wt. Rayons

Because of Sulky's silky finish and legendary quality, it will smoothly glide through a quilt top, batting and backing when stitched either by hand or machine. Sulky Rayon does _not_ fray and fuzz in the machine, and it does _not_ shrink like cotton can. It is cross-wound on the small spool to ensure easier thread flow on any machine, and consistently superior stitch quality. It is easy to identify the color numbers and weight sizes because they are printed in black ink on each small snap-end spool. **Sulky 40 wt. Rayon is completely colorfast** and machine washable in either hot or cold water. Use a laundry soap or detergent that

DOES NOT contain chlorine or optical brighteners. It is also dry cleanable. Sulky Rayon is a man-made fiber that has very much the same luster as silk, and silk's smoothness, but it is stronger and less costly than silk thread.

All Sulky Rayon threads are made in Germany exclusively from German-made Enka fibers, proven to be the highest quality rayon/viscose fibers in the world. Visit www.sulky.com to see the proof. You can create with confidence because of Sulky's consistently high quality.

Sulky Rayon is Color-Fast.

Sulky 40 wt. Rayon is universally used for computerized machine embroidery because most designs are digitized for it. Sulky is the first choice of home embroiderers because of its excellent runability, unparalleled quality, and huge selection of 388 colors. Sulky 40 wt. Rayon is also easier to use than polyester because it has less stretch and stretch memory which causes less puckering than with polyester thread.

Sulky Rayon lays down nicely in the design without the occasional thread pull-ups which occur when using polyester. Sulky 40 wt. Rayon's look is more soft, warm and natural compared to the almost "plasticky" look of polyester. And, polyester's added, unnecessary strength causes the acceleration of wear on the machine's moving parts and thread path. Because Sulky 40 wt. is available in 333 solid colors and 55 variegated and multi-colors on 250 yard snap-end spools, 850 yard snap-end King spools and 5,500 yard snap-end Jumbo Cones, it is also the thread of choice for quilters who love to add embroidery to their quilts.

No wonder our 40 wt. rayon threads are the strongest, most elegant rayon threads available.

There's more to selecting the right 40 wt. rayon thread than meets the eye—without a microscope that is. You see, while the viscose that all rayon threads are made from comes from trees, the trees that ENKA's raw, viscose fibers are made from are better. That's because ENKA trees are grown for twenty years in optimal climactic and geological conditions. Only the highest quality, long-chain cellulose fibers are reprocessed from these trees. And only those fibers are used for Sulky Rayon Threads. That's why you experience less breakage with Sulky/ENKA threads, even when using high-speed embroidery machines. And why everything you make using Sulky/ENKA threads lasts longer and looks better years from now. And why embroidery connoisseurs prefer the softer, warmer, more natural look of Sulky Rayon Thread. Granted, all this may not be apparent when you're just looking at a 40 wt. rayon thread. But put Sulky/ENKA fibers and the competition's under a microscope and you'll see what we're talking about.

Express yourself with sulky®

Decorative Thread, Stabilizers & Books

Sulky Metallics

Doll by: Julie McCullough
Magic Threads™
www.magicthreads.com

Holoshimmer™

Add some sparkle to your quilting with this brilliantly reflective thread. It is a flat, ribbon-like thread that is strong for a metallic. It sews easily following the tips below.

• Available in 24 colors.
• 250 yd. snap-end spool.
• 3mm length recommended for best reflectiveness.

Sulky Sliver™

A flat, ribbon-like, polyester film that is metallized with aluminum to make it very reflective. It is slightly thinner than Holoshimmer.

• Available in 24 colors.
• 250 yd. snap-end spool.
• 3mm length recommended for best reflectiveness.

Tips:

1. Use at least a 14/90 Metallic Needle or Topstitch Needle.
2. Use Holoshimmer and Sliver only on a vertical spool pin with a felt pad underneath.
3. Choose slow to medium speed.
4. Lower the top tension a lot.
5. Use with Sulky Bobbin Thread, Sulky Invisible or 40 wt. Rayon in the bobbin.
6. Iron at low temperature from the wrong side.
7. Washable or dry cleanable.

Original Metallic

• Available in 36 brilliant solid and multi-colors.
• 165 yd. size snap-end spool.
• A round, twisted thread wrapped with the finest metallic foil around a strong core to produce a soft, smooth thread.
• Follow the Tips for successful results.

Sulky Poly Deco™ and Sulky Premium Invisible

Poly Deco™

is a top quality, strong, 100% polyester thread that has a special finish that makes it shiny. It is especially suited for embroidery on children's clothing, sports clothes, or anything that might be washed frequently in warm to hot water using detergents that contain bleach or optical brighteners.

Since Poly Deco has more stretch and stretch memory than rayon, the top tension generally needs to be reduced, and the type and amount of stabilizer(s) can be different than when using rayon.

- 40 wt. is available in 138 colors, including 8 neon colors on a 250 yd. snap-end spool, a 900 yd. snap-end King spool, and a 5,500 yd. snap-end Jumbo Cone.

- Great for hand sewing bindings and invisible applique.

Sulky Polyester Invisible™

Wonderful as a lightweight, very fine .004 monofilament bobbin thread. Soft and plyable enough for baby quilts.

Great for:
- *Machine "hand-look" quilting, stitching-in-the-ditch and invisible applique.*

Available in:
- *Smoke for dark fabrics and clear for light fabrics.*
- *440 yd. snap-end spools and 2,400 yd. snap-end King spools.*

Tips:

1. *Wind onto bobbins using a slow speed.*
2. *Compatible with all Sulky threads.*
3. *Iron on low heat.*

Adding Borders

Think of adding borders as the frame to your patchwork artistry. Borders should accentuate the color and design of the quilt. They complete the theme of the quilt and give the eye a stopping point. The border can be the crowning glory of the quilt. Allow yourself to step outside of the box!

Yardage is based on a crosswise cut. Measure and pin carefully to prevent stretching. If needed, join the 42" strips together by lining up the fabric strips as shown below, then stitching diagonally across. Trim to 1/4" and press open for less bulk.

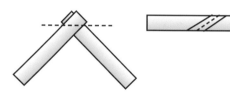

Horizontal Borders

1. Find the center point in each of the four sides of the quilt top and mark each one with a pin.

Center of border strip

Length of quilt at center

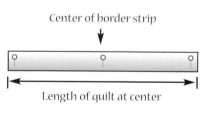

2. Measure the quilt down the center, from top to bottom. Cut two strips to this measurement. Mark the center of each strip with a pin. Match the centers of the strips with the centers of the sides. Pin the entire strips in place, then sew them onto the quilt top. Press the seams toward the borders.

3. Measure the quilt across the center, from side to side, including the side borders. Cut two strips to this measurement. Mark the center of each strip with a pin.

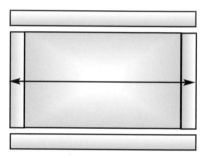

4. Match the centers of the strips with the centers of the top and bottom, then sew these strips onto the quilt top. Press seams toward the borders.

Cornerstones

1. On each of the four sides of the quilt top, find the center point and mark it with a pin.

2. Measure the quilt across the center, from side to side. Cut two strips to this measurement. Sew a corner square equal to the width of your border onto both ends of each strip. (For instance, to a 6" x 42" border, add a 6" square on each end.) Press seams toward the border. Mark the center of each strip with a pin and set it aside.

3. Measure the quilt down the center, from top to bottom. Cut two strips to this measurement. Mark the center of each strip with a pin. Match the centers of the strips with the centers of the sides, then sew a strip onto each side of the quilt top. Press the seams toward the borders.

4. Sew the corner square strips onto the top and bottom of the quilt top, matching the center pins and corner square seams.

Mitered Borders

1. Measure the length and width of the top through the center.

2. Have enough fabric for all four sides of the borders to equal the measured width of the quilt top, plus the width of the border on each end, plus another 6" to 12", times 2. Repeat for the length of the quilt top.

In this example, the width of our top measures 20" through the center, plus a 4" border on each end, plus 6" to 12", which equals at least 34".

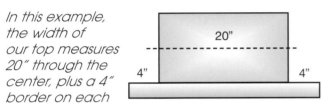

3. Cut the border fabric into strips the desired width. If the fabric is cut across the width of the yardage, it may need to be pieced diagonally to achieve the desired length.

4. Mark the center of each border piece with a pin after you fold it in half cross-wise. Also, mark the center of all four sides of the quilt top.

Center of Border Strip

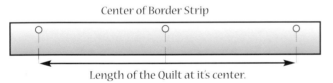

Length of the Quilt at it's center.

5. Match the centers of the first border and side, and attach the border by starting to sew a quarter inch in from the edge of the quilt top. Backstitch. Sew the seam. Stop a quarter inch from the end. Backstitch again. Do not catch the fabric edge of the adjoining border in the backstitch. Repeat for the other three borders.

6. Press the seams toward the outer borders. At this point, you will have extra fabric at all corners.

7. Lay out the quilt top on a flat surface, with the wrong side facing up. Use a 12-1/2" square ruler to mark a 45° line from the inside corner to the outside corner – as illustrated above.

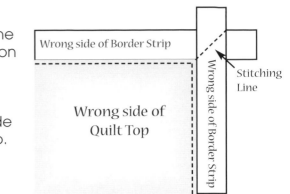

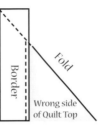

8. Fold the side border back at the marked line. Press a crease along the fold while maintaining a true 45° angle. Spray Sulky KK 2000 Temporary Spray Adhesive between the fabrics to ensure secure placement. Fold the fabric out of the way to be able to stitch inside the crease. Begin stitching 1/4" away from the corner.

Border Tips:

1. *If you're having problems getting the borders to lay flat, purchase extra border fabric and cut them from the more stable lengthwise grain.*

2. *Stripes make exciting borders. Try the mitered border for a real "framed" look.*

3. *Directional fabrics require more yardage to allow for design placement. Some designs must stand upright and must be cut both on the crosswise grain and the lengthwise grain to achieve a uniform appearance.*

4. *Pieced borders, if not sewn accurately, can be troublesome. Slight inaccuracies in cutting, piecing or pressing may cause them not to fit the quilt center. Check the seam allowances first and correct them if possible. As a last resort, make adjustments easily by taking in or letting out 1/8" seam allowances. Each 1/8" adjustment will result in a 1/4" size change in the border. Place these adjustments throughout the length of the border, as needed.*

Making a "Quilt Sandwich"

■ Marking the Quilt Top

If using quilting stencils, mark your quilt top with them now. A dark fabric needs a light marking pencil or chalk. A light fabric needs a dark chalk. Clover makes a great set of three chalk pencils, blue, pink and white, which wash out beautifully. Of course, test them on each fabric before using, and always

Sulky Fabri-Solvy
Quilting Pattern

wash the quilt before ironing over any marked lines. Never use ink pens or regular pencils because the marks can become permanent.

Consider these alternative methods of marking a quilt. Mark the quilt pattern on either Fabri-Solvy or Tear-Easy Stabilizer instead of marking directly on the quilt top and wondering if the direct marks will wash out or reappear. Any of the Sulky Stabilizers can be temporarily adhered to the quilt with Sulky KK 2000 Temporary Spray Adhesive.

Try "Quilting Made Easy" and "Borders Made Easy"- adhesive paper quilting stencils, as well as household items such as cups, cookie cutters, or plates. Even leaves from a backyard can yield interesting quilting designs.

Marking Tips:

1. Spray Sulky KK 2000 on the back of a stencil to keep it from shifting while you mark the fabric. KK 2000 will make it repositionable and, if exposed to air, will dissipate from the stencil in a day or two.
2. Create original tissue paper stencils by tracing quilting designs onto them. Spray the back with Sulky KK 2000. Place on the quilt and stitch through the paper. Remove when the quilting is done!
3. Trace quilting designs onto Sulky Fabri-Solvy as pictured to the left using a water soluble marker. After stitching simply wash the quilt and the Fabri-Solvy is gone leaving only your quilting. Fast and easy!
4. To help keep the fabric from moving while marking by hand, place a board covered with fine sandpaper under the fabric.

■ Batting

There are many manufacturers and types of Batting:
• Cotton • Wool • Silk • Polyester Blends, and they each have different qualities and loft that need to be considered for each quilting project. Quilter's Dream Cotton or Poly can be quilted up to 8" apart. It will not shift or gravitate through the quilt top as some poor quality battings are prone to do. Ultra or High Loft battings are only suitable for tied quilts. Usually Low Loft is best for machine quilting.

Always allow the batting to breathe and relax overnight if it has been taken out of a plastic bag where it has been tightly doubled and rolled to take up the least space in a store.

Backing Fabric

The quilt back must be a few inches larger all around than the finished quilt top. If needed, cut and piece your backing fabric to size.

Making a Traditional "Quilt Sandwich"

1. Smooth the backing fabric, right side down, onto a large surface like a quilting table or ping-pong table. To prevent shifting, secure it with either masking tape or binder clips. It should be smooth and taut, but not stretched.

2. Lay the batting on top of it. Smooth in place. Fold half of the batting back to expose the backing. Lightly spray the backing fabric with Sulky KK 2000. Carefully smooth the batting back into place. Repeat for the other half.

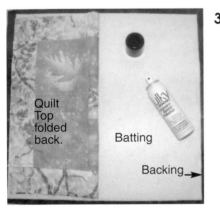

Quilt Top folded back.

Batting

Backing →

3. Place the quilt top (right side up) on top of the batting. Fold half of the top back to expose the batting. Lightly spray KK 2000 on the folded half of the quilt top. Carefully smooth the top back into place. Repeat for the other half.

4. Secure all layers of the quilt sandwich to a large, flat surface with masking tape, or use binder clips every 12" to 15".

5. On large quilts, pin every 12" in all directions using 1" brass or nickel-plated quilter's safety pins. Avoid stainless steel pins as they may rust and ruin the quilt. Remove the tape or binder clips and get ready to quilt.

Stitch, Turn and Tie Method

1. Smooth the batting onto a large surface like a cutting table or ping-pong table; secure it using either masking tape, binder clips or whatever works best to prevent shifting. Do **not stretch** the batting. It should be taut and smooth.

2. Layer the quilt back (right side up) on top of the batting and smooth it into place (taut, not stretched). Fold up half of the quilt back to expose the batting. Lightly spray the backing fabric with Sulky KK-2000. Carefully smooth the backing fabric into place. Repeat for the other half.

3. Finally, place the quilt top (wrong side up) on the top of this "Quilt Sandwich". Loosely pin 1" from the edge, all around, using quilter's safety pins.

4. Remove the masking tape or binders. Stitch around the edges of the quilt, leaving a 12" opening. Leave a 1/2" seam allowance as you trim away any excess batting or backing. Turn the quilt right side out through the opening. Hand whip-stitch the opening closed.

5. Lay the quilt on your large surface again to smooth it out. Put safety pins where you expect to tie it, about five ties per block. Thread three or more strands of Sulky 12 weight Cotton Thread through a hand-sewing tapestry needle. You now have six strands to stitch with.

6. Using the pin as a mark, stitch from the front to the back, then take one more stitch from the back to the front. Repeat the stitching to secure. Tie a double knot on the front and trim the ties to 1/2" long. Remove pins.

29

Quilting the Top

Insert a new needle in the sewing machine with every project and every quilting job. A quilting or top-stitch needle is designed to protect the thread with a deeper scarf (the channel on the front of the needle that runs to the eye) and a larger eye. It is coated to prevent the batting from being pulled up through the fabric. The sharp point gives a clear, concise stitch.

Quilting serves several functions. First, of course, is to hold the quilt together. Second, the quilted nooks and crannies catch body warmth and hold it. Third, it adds beauty to the design of the quilt. And finally, the more a quilt is quilted, the longer it will endure. Lessons learned from antique quilts prove that intensive quilting greatly extends the life of a quilt. Many antique quilts that were quilted 1/4" apart have endured many generations of use and love.

There are two options for machine quilting: machine-fed or free-motion.

In this section we will explore these two options and which is the best to use for different quilting techniques.

stitch or setting the stitch length on the longest straight stitch setting. Or, baste using a free-motion stitch, moving the fabric rapidly to create long, straight stitches. But the preferred method is to pin-baste using large quilter's safety pins.

On large quilts, pin at least every 12" in all directions, using 1" quilter's safety pins. Avoid stainless steel pins as they can rust in humid climates and ruin the quilt.

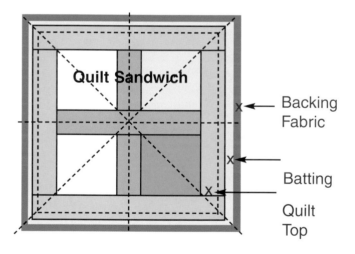

Quilt Sandwich

Backing Fabric

Batting

Quilt Top

Basting - Long, running stitches.

It is imperative that the layers (backing, batting and quilt top) are basted together before any quilting is done. You can use KK 2000 Temporary Spray Adhesive to hold layers together for basting. Baste either by hand, or by making long, running stitches with a high-contrast thread on the machine, selecting either the basting

Many quilters choose to have their larger quilts basted on a long-arm quilting machine. Look in the yellow pages of your telephone book to find a long-arm quilter near you, or check with your local quilt shop. A long-arm quilting machine is a professional, high-speed, straight stitch machine with a large table that allows you to layer your quilt and keep it taut while quilting. Many of the sewing machine manufacturers have introduced very reasonably priced short-arm quilting machines for home use.

Quilting "In the Ditch"

1. "Walking Foot" or "Even-feed Foot"
The walking foot feeds the top fabric through the machine, while the feed dogs (teeth) feed the bottom fabric. Without a walking foot, the quilt sandwich can pucker and bunch up. It's a must for straight-line quilting. Some machines have an integrated dual feed system and don't need this accessory.

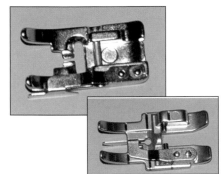

2. "Edge Foot"
Adjust the needle position to quilt an even distance from a seam. Also great for "Stitching in the Ditch" or seam line.

3. "Ditch Foot" - "Stitching-in-the-Ditch"
This is a relatively new foot only available on newer model machines.

"Stitching in the Ditch" is a quilting term that means stitching in the low side of the seam line. When seams are pressed to one side, they form a ridge or high side. The low side is referred to as the ditch. This technique is usually recommended for beginners, and is frequently done with either Sulky Premium Invisible thread, Sulky Holoshimmer™, Sliver™, or other Sulky Metallic on the top, and a Sulky Cotton thread in the bobbin that matches the back of the quilt. Most other invisible thread is not recommended for baby projects, but Sulky Invisible Thread is soft, supple and gentle against the skin.

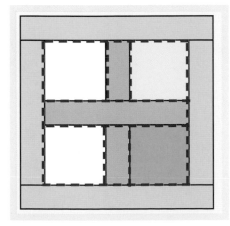

Besides adding to the look of the quilt, this stitching also acts as "stay stitching" to keep the quilt top from getting distorted and stretched out of shape when more quilting is added. For best results, place your hands on both sides of the seam and apply slight outward pressure which will make the seam open up and lay flatter. Some quilts lend themselves to only quilting in the ditch, especially when you want your piecing to "pop". Since we prefer to see the thread on our quilts, Holoshimmer, which comes in 24 sparkling colors, adds some subtle glimmer to quilts without overwhelming them with glitz. But if you do not want the stitch-in-the-ditch thread to show, use Sulky Premium Polyester Invisible Thread in clear or smoke.

4. Only use the best quality threads for your quilts. In the past, most quilts were only quilted with 100% cotton thread. Today, we have many other choices that provide us with artistic license. Choose a Sulky thread to complement the design and color of your quilt. A quilt destined for heavy use will require a more durable thread such as Sulky premium quality 12 wt. or 30 wt, 100% Egyptian long-staple cotton. Most threads look best quilted at a 2.5 or 2mm stitch length. However, when quilting with Sulky Metallic Threads, we recommend a stitch length of 3.0, when possible, to show more reflection.

5. Start and stop a line of quilting by holding the fabric in place while stitching three or four stitches in place. This replaces tieing a knot as you would in hand quilting.

"Machine-Fed" Quilting

Using an even-feed foot is suggested to help the machine feed the bulky quilt sandwich with the same action on the top of the quilt as the feed teeth are doing on the under side of the quilt, giving you an even length to all stitches.

There are many times when having the machine feeding the fabric will be the preferred method for quilting. Some of them are:

- When quilting from corner to corner in a block as on the tablecloth on page 49.
- Stitching the Greek Key design as on the Marine Biology Quilt on page 96.
- Cross Hatch quilting using the quilting guide bar as on the Kitchen Goodies toaster and blender covers on page 126.
- When echo quilting as on the Christmas Angel Mantle Cover on page 112.
- When following a simple continuous line pattern. Some machines even have machine-fed stipple stitching that looks like free-motion.

Set up the Machine for Machine-Fed Quilting

- Feed Dogs UP: Machine feeding.
- Straight Stitch: Center needle position.
- Stitch Length: 2 - 2.5 so the stitch is long enough to show off the thread.
- Place appropriate foot on the machine.
- Test top tension and adjust if needed so that no bobbin thread is pulled up when stitching.
- Always lock your stitches when you begin stitching and when you intend to cut the thread.
- Use a slow to medium speed.
- Select needle down position, if available.
- Begin by stitching slowly until you get comfortable. It is always best to use a practice quilt sandwich before working on your quilt.

Quilting Tips:

1. Quilting gloves can give the extra grip you need to move the fabric while minimizing the strain on your hands.
2. To control the bulk, roll the quilt from both sides toward the center. Start quilting in the center and work toward one side, unrolling as needed.
3. To help keep control, always stop with the needle down in the fabric.
4. Look ahead of the work, not at the needle. Know where the quilting is going. Make sure it isn't falling off the machine table since extra drag on the quilt will effect the stitching. Always make sure you have the space to move the quilt around without obstructions.
5. Relaxation tapes or a glass of wine may help keep the quilting smooth and enjoyable.
6. Stop every 10 –15 minutes, stand up, stretch and rotate your shoulders.
7. Posture and breathing are important for successful quilting. Try the "Body Rite - the Posture Pleaser™" by Mageyes. It really helps to hold the shoulders in place and reduces upper back strain.
8. Try the "Sew Slip-Free Motion Sheet" to help the quilt glide over the bed of the machine.

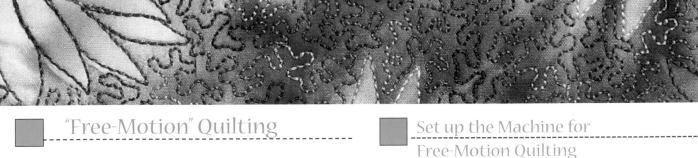

"Free-Motion" Quilting

The term "free-hand" or "free-motion" quilting refers to stitching with the machine feed dogs, or feed teeth, lowered or covered, and a specialty foot attached that hops up and down allowing the quilter to freely move the fabric beneath the foot. You, as the quilter, actually take over the action of the feed dogs. The stitch length is determined by how fast you move the fabric along with how fast you run the machine. Practice on a scrap quilt sandwich until you feel you have adequate control.

How you move the hoop or quilt sandwich determines the look of the stitches. You are the controlling factor. Set the machine for a straight stitch, zero width, and move the hoop from side to side or up and down. If you move the hoop quickly while running the machine at the same moderate to fast speed, you will have long stitches. If you move the hoop slower, the stitches will be shorter in length.

In 1981, Joyce Drexler wrote a book entitled, "THREAD PAINTING - MAKING APPLIQUES OF THREAD". Recently Joyce has written an updated and greatly expanded version of this book for Sulky of America entitled: "Sulky Secrets to Successful Embroidery" Book 900B-15.

While most sewing machine instruction books have a basic section on how to properly set up the sewing machine for "free-motion" work, in Sulky's 168 page embroidery book, you can learn free-motion embroidery, step-by-step, with colored photos and easy-to-understand descriptions.

Set up the Machine for Free-Motion Quilting

1. Use a clean, well-tuned zig-zag Sewing Machine.
2. Lower or cover your feed dogs. If you do not have a way to drop the feed dogs or cover them, tape an index card over them.
3. Remove the presser foot and screw; place them in the attachment box. Attach the appropriate darning or quilting foot on the machine.
4. Engage the needle-down function if your machine has this feature. (Most quilters find this feature to be the single most valuable upgrade on a new sewing machine.)
5. Insert a new 14/90 topstitch needle.
6. The stitch length is now controlled entirely by a combination of how fast you run the machine and how fast you move the fabric. Some machines have a stitch regulator that actually keeps your free-motion stitches evenly spaced.
7. Select a moderate to fast speed. Steady machine speed and steady movement of the fabric are essential to successful, even quilting.
8. Select a straight stitch for quilting or thread sketching. You will not want the bobbin thread to ever show on the quilt top. To prevent this from happening, use Sulky Clear or Smoke Invisible Thread in the bobbin, or the same type and color thread in the bobbin as in the needle. You may need to slightly lower your top tension.

If you have never pieced or quilted before, try the Beginner Quilt Sampler on page 36.

Free-motion quilting designs are generally curved and continuous line designs such as feathers, cables, stippling and circles.

"Free-Motion" Quilting

1. Before free-motion quilting any project, always "warm up" on a practice quilt sandwich to loosen up tight arms and hands. Thread tension can be checked and adjusted on this practice piece.

2. Start and stop each line of stitching by letting the needle go up and down several times while only slightly moving the fabric, forming a knot. This knot is less obvious than back-tacking, and less time-consuming than hand knotting. (Automatic tie-off is another good feature to look for in a new sewing machine.)

3. Cut off all loose threads, top and bottom, before moving from one area of quilting to another. Be careful not to clip the fabric. Many machines have an automatic thread cutter which eliminates this possibility.

4. Now is the time to embellish with Sulky specialty threads. Choose a thread that complements the color and theme of the quilt (like Sulky 12 wt. or 30 wt. Cotton Blendables featured in the header on this page) and have fun. Quilting and embellishing are as much a creative part of the quilt as the fabric choice and patchwork. Try a shiny Sulky Rayon or glitzy Sulky Metallic Thread to add pizzazz and individuality to the piece.

5. Start in the center of the quilt top and work out to the edges. Any "excess" fullness can be eased outward.

Feet used for free-motion quilting. Most hop up and down allowing you to move the fabric.

The term *"Stipple Quilting"* refers to free-motion straight stitching done in smaller, soft, curvy, puzzle-like shapes. Lines of stitching do not normally intersect or touch. It is a preferred quilting method for small, open areas on quilts.

Note the example of stippling using the purple Blendable stitching in the border above.

The term *"Meandering Quilting"* refers to "free-motion" straight stitching done in large, soft, curvy, puzzle-piece-like shapes. Lines of stitching normally do not intersect or touch. It is a preferred quilting method for large open areas on quilts.

See example below:

Hand Quilting
by Nancy Bryant

Suggested Supplies:
- Text: *"That Perfect Stitch"*
  by Roxanne McElroy
- Quilting Hoop or Q-Snap Quilting Frame
- Roxanne Thimble to fit the middle finger
  of the hand that holds the needle
- Thread snips or small scissors
- Quilting Needles: Size 10 Richard
  Hemmings Betweens
- Quilting Thread: Sulky 12 wt.
  Cotton Blendables
- Sulky KK 2000 to Baste the quilt
- Thread Heaven™ Thread
  Conditioner and Protectant
- Clover® Double Needle Threader
- Muslin Backing
- Dream Poly Batting
- Hand Quilting Hoop - optional

Create the Quilt Stitch

1. Thread an 18" length of Sulky 12 wt. Cotton Blendables, or Sulky 12 wt. Cotton thread in a Size10 Richard Hemmings Quilting needle.
2. Coat the entire length of the thread in Thread Heaven thread conditioner.
3. Tie a quilter's knot in the end of the thread. Wrap the end of the thread several times around the tip of the needle and pull the thread through, as if making a French Knot.
4. Place a Roxanne's Thimble on the middle finger of your quilting hand.
5. Stitch toward your body.
6. Insert the needle in the top layer of the fabric and gently pull until the knot disappears under the surface of the fabric.
7. Bring up the needle at the start of the first stitch.
8. Place one hand under the quilt and place your finger under the spot planned for the first stitch.
9. Place the needle perpendicular to the fabric and push just until the tip of the needle touches the finger under the quilt.
10. Rock the needle down and press gently until the needle tip just barely appears on the quilt top.
11. Rock the needle back up, and press gently, just until the needle touches the under finger. Repeat until several stitches are on the needle. Pull through.
12. To end a line of quilting, tie another tiny quilter's knot and pop it through the fabric.

Evenly spaced, uniform stitches are more important than tiny stitches. Stitches should be the same size on the top and back of the quilt. Knots should never be seen on the top of the quilt.

A Beginner "Free-Motion" Quilting Sampler

Inside the quilt image:

Border **C**

A #1 Meandering

B Sashing

A #2 Circles/Bubbles

B Sashing

C

B Sashing

A #3 Small Stippling

B Sashing

A #4 Leaf Quilting Design

Border **C**

Border **C** (left and right)

Fabrics & Supplies Needed for Quilt:

All strips are cut across the fabric, selvage to selvage, assuming 42" of usable fabric. Cut off all selvages.

✢ Fabric A - (4) 5" squares
✢ Fabric B - (1) 2-1/2" x 42" strip for sashing;
   Cut this into (4) 5" strips.
✢ Fabric C - (2) 2-1/4" x 42" strips. From one,
   cut (1) 2-1/2 square; remainder is for border.
✢ (2) 10" x 15" pieces for slip-cover pillow back
✢ (2) 18" squares of Sulky Soft 'n Sheer Stabilizer
✢ (1) 15" Pillow Form
✢ (1) 18" square of muslin for practice piece
✢ (2) 18" squares of Warm and Natural Batting
✢ Sulky Threads - Invisible, 30 wt. & 40 wt. Rayon,
   Holoshimmer, 12 wt. & 30 wt. Blendables
✢ Machine needle sizes: 14/90 and 16/100
✢ Machine feet: 1/4", Stitch-in-the-Ditch,
   Stippling or Free-motion Quilting
✢ General sewing supplies - see page 3

This project is the perfect beginner exercise to learn basic piecing, assembly of a quilt top, as well as the proper preparation for quilting by using a smaller pillow top in a streamlined learning process. We will cover 4 different styles of "free-motion" quilting, add more blocks for more quilting techniques, and make it a tablerunner if you want to! Or make 2 coordinating pillows.

Credits:

Level: Beginner
Designed by:
   Joyce Drexler
Fabrics: Fossil Fern™
   by Benartex® and
   Butterfly Print by
   Timeless Treasures®

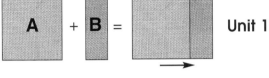

Step 1: Piece the "Quilt Top" (Pillow Top)

A "Quilt Top" is usually made up of pieced fabrics which form a pattern that is the top layer of a quilt. Many of us say we are "quilters", but technically, we are "piecers". Many quilters never graduate to the quilting process, but prefer the challenge of piecing quilt patterns, then sending their quilt tops to someone else to hand quilt or machine quilt. _But you can do it!_ It's easy and fun following these simple directions!

- Attach the 1/4" Foot   • Select straight stitch, center position, length 2.
- Insert a 14/90 Quilting Machine Needle   • Thread the top and bobbin with
    Sulky 30 wt. Cotton Thread in a neutral beige or medium gray.
- Press seams in the directions the arrows indicate - toward the Sashing Strips B.

1. Using a 1/4" seam allowance through-out, sew a sashing strip "B" to fabric block "A", forming Unit 1.

2. Sew another fabric block "A" to Unit 1, forming Unit 2.

3. Repeat 1 above, forming Unit 3.

4. Repeat 2 above, forming Unit 4.

5. Sew sashing strip "B" to fabric square "C". Sew that unit to another sashing strip "B". Then sew the completed sashing strip to Unit 2, forming Unit 5.

6. Sew remaining Unit 4 to Unit 5, forming Unit 6.

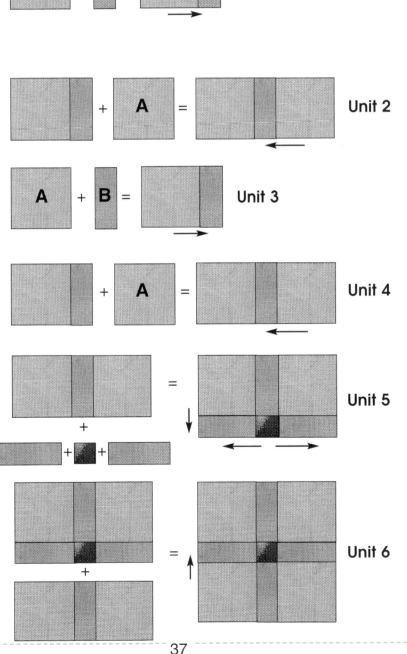

7. Measure vertically down the center of Unit 6 and cut 2 border strips "C" that measurement. Sew them to each side of Unit 6, forming Unit 7. Press seams toward the borders.

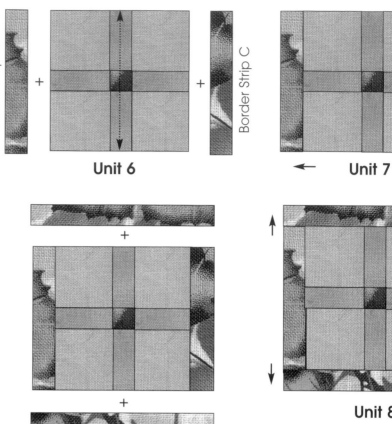

Border Strip C

+

Border Strip C

+

Unit 6

← **Unit 7** →

8. Measure horizontally across the center of Unit 7 and cut 2 border strips "C" that measurement. Sew them to the top and bottom of Unit 7, forming Unit 8, which is now the finished "Pillow Top". Press toward the borders.

+

+

Unit 8
The finished Quilt Top (Pillow Top).

By measuring vertically and horizontally down and across the center of a quilt, cutting border strips to that measurement, and easing (if necessary) the strips onto the quilt top, your quilt will hang straight, without wavy edges. See page 26 for additional information.

Step 2: Prepare the Quilt Sandwich for Quilting - see page 28.

Make a Practice Quilt Sandwich substituting muslin for the Pillow Top.

Step 3: Baste the Quilt Sandwich - see page 30.

Step 4: Quilting In the Ditch - see page 31.

Refer to the "Quick Thread Reference Guide to using Sulky Threads" on page 16.

1. Wind a bobbin in the color of the backing fabric or use Sulky Premium Invisible Thread.
   Note: Always wind invisible thread onto a plastic bobbin slowly. Any monofilament thread can stretch if wound too fast and can actually break a plastic bobbin or cause it to be difficult to remove from the bobbin winder. It will certainly affect your thread tension. We recommend only winding the bobbin half full with invisible thread.

2. For quilting "in-the-ditch", insert a 14/90 Metallic or Topstitch needle and thread the top with Sulky Holoshimmer™ Metallic Thread #6007.
   Note: Holoshimmer Thread should only be placed on a <u>vertical</u> spool pin with a felt pad under it. It is a flat thread and the twisting action when unwinding off a horizontal spool pin can cause breakage. Holoshimmer is available in 24 luscious colors.

3. There are actual stitch-in-the-ditch machine feet available now for some model machines that are designed to help you stitch right down the seam line. While some people like to use a zipper foot or edge foot, a clear foot with a center needle position mark will help you in stitching right on the seam.

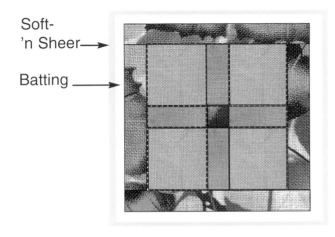

Soft-'n Sheer→

Batting →

4. **Select:**
   - Feed Dogs UP: Machine Feeding
   - Straight Stitch: Center Position
   - Stitch Length: 2.5 to 3.0 so the stitch is long enough to show off the reflectiveness of the Holoshimmer.
   - Reduce top tension enough so that no bobbin thread is pulled up when stitching.
   - Attach the stitch-in-the-ditch foot.
   - Always lock your stitches when you begin stitching and when you stop to cut the thread.
   - Use a slow to medium speed.

5. Begin by stitching slowly until you are comfortable staying on the seam line. Stitch all seam lines as shown in the above illustration.

 Quilting Exercise 1: "Free-Motion" - Meandering - read page 34.

1. Thread the top with a Sulky 30 wt. Cotton Blendable. Slowly wind a bobbin with Sulky Premium Clear Invisible Thread or the same Sulky 30 wt. Cotton Blendable.

2. Always use a size 14/90 quilting or topstitch needle with Sulky 30 wt. Cotton Blendable Thread. (Joyce used color #4020.)

3. There are free-motion quilting feet available for most machines. They often look like a small hoop. Some have a horseshoe shape with an open front. These feet usually have a bar that goes over the needle thumb screw, and they hop up and down instead of holding the fabric down all the time like regular presser feet. Look under Darning or Free-Motion in your machine instruction book to see what foot is recommended and how to properly attach it to the machine.

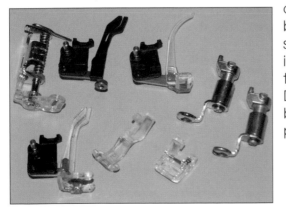

4. **For "Free-Motion":**
    - Feed Dogs DOWN or covered.
    - Straight Stitch: Center position.
    - Slightly reduce top tension so that no bobbin thread shows on top.
    - Always lock your stitches when you begin stitching and before you cut the thread.
    - Sew at a slow to medium speed.
    - Sit so that your nose is in line with the needle. Rest your forearms on the table in front of the machine.
    - Hold on to the quilt sandwich or place it in a machine embroidery hoop. If using a hoop, keep your fingers on the outside of the hoop rings.
    - Breathe. Relax your arms and only move the fabric or hoop with your fingers.

5. Make a practice quilt sandwich, substituting muslin for the Pillow Top. Always practice the suggested quilting stitch before working on your Pillow Top. Stitch your project on the top left square in Section "1" using a Meandering Quilting Stitch.

A great follow-up project to this Beginner Sampler would be the quilted pillows with various finishes, starting on page 51.

Quilting Exercise 2

"Free-Motion" - Circles/Bubbles

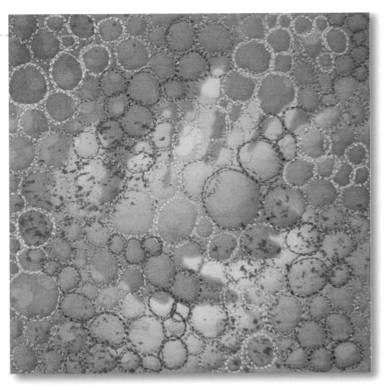

1. In the bobbin, put Sulky Clear Invisible or a 30 wt. Rayon that matches the top thread. (Joyce used Sulky 30 wt. Rayon - #2114.)

2. Use the same needle and quilting foot that you used in Exercise 1.

3. Practice on your scrap quilt sandwich. Make large circles and small circles as shown to the right. You can go over the circles once, twice, or several times, depending on the look you want to achieve. Experiment until you feel comfortable, and then stitch on your Sampler in Section 2, the top right square of the Pillow Top.

See how effective the circle quilting technique can be as shown in this close-up of the Quilt titled "Marine Biology". It was quilted using Sulky Sliver. Learn how to piece this quilt on page 96.

Quilting Exercise 3: "Free-Motion" Stippling

The term "Stipple Quilting" refers to "free-motion" straight stitching done in small, soft, curvy, puzzle-like shapes. Lines of stitching do not intersect or touch. It is a preferred quilting method for small, open areas on quilts.

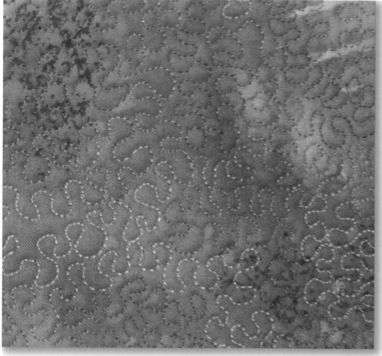

1. Wind a bobbin in the color of Sulky 40 wt. Rayon that matches the top thread, or use Sulky Premium Invisible Thread. (Joyce used Sulky 40 wt. Rayon #2114.)

2. Use the same needle as in Exercise 1.

3. Use the same Quilting Foot that you used in previous exercises.

4. Adjust the top tension so that no bobbin thread shows on the top.

5. Practice on your scrap quilt sandwich. Experiment until you feel comfortable, and then stitch your Sampler in Section 3, the bottom left square of thePillow Top, as shown to the right.

Virtually all Sulky threads are now available on Jumbo Cones.

Quilting Exercise 4: "Free-motion" over a Solvy™ Template

Any of the Solvys are perfect quilt design template material. Sulky Water Soluble Stabilizers for this use come in various choices: Original Solvy, Super Solvy, Ultra Solvy, and Fabri-Solvy.

These amazing products make following any quilting design so easy, with no fear of leaving reappearing marks on your quilt top. (Joyce used the quilt design "Evelyn's Meandering Leaves" found on page 44.) Lightly spray KK-2000 onto a piece of Super Solvy to hold it in place while you trace the quilting pattern with a permanent ink or water soluble marker. Then smooth it over the quilt top and it will stay in place while you quilt over it, following the lines. When you have completed the stitching, dissipate the KK 2000 if it still remains tacky (KK 2000 is not water soluble.) by pressing with a warm dry iron, or tumbling in a dryer for a few minutes before you immerse it in water. The Super Solvy disappears, leaving only your beautiful quilting behind. *It's like magic!*

1. Wind a bobbin with a Sulky 30 wt. Blendable that matches the top thread, or use Sulky Premium Invisible Thread.

2. Change to a size 16/100 top-stitch needle. (Joyce used 12 wt. Cotton Blendable #4020.) If your machine does not like the heavier 12 wt. for free-motion work, substitute Sulky 30 wt. Cotton or Rayon.

3. Use the same free-motion quilting foot.

4. Adjust the top tension so that no bobbin thread shows on top.

5. Practice on your scrap quilt sandwich. Experiment until you feel comfortable, and then stitch your sampler in Section 4, the bottom right square of the Pillow Top, as shown above right.

6. This continuous-line pattern can also be stitched without a pattern once you become familiar with the direction and flow.

See how beautifully this quilting stitch using Blendables enhanced the pillow above.

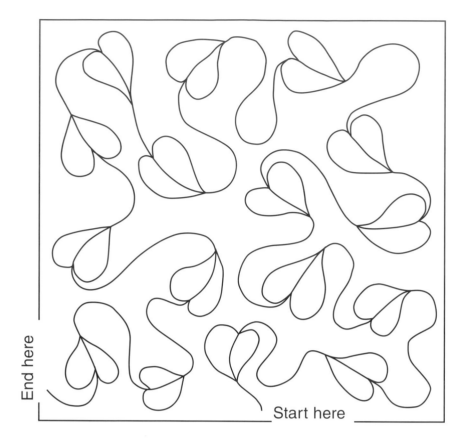

End here

Start here

"Meandering Leaves" Quilting Pattern

This continuous-line quilting design that was developed by Evelyn Byler is one of our favorites.

Trace the design onto Solvy or Super Solvy using a fine-line, permanent-ink marker or water soluble marker.

Once you are comfortable with the movement creating the leaves, you will be able to stitch this pattern on your own without using a traced pattern.

Without   With

Exercise 5: "Free-motion" Outline Quilting

1. Use a bobbin half filled with Sulky Premium Invisible Thread.

2. Change your needle to a 14/90 topstitch needle. (Joyce used Sulky Sliver #8006. You could use Sulky Holoshimmer if you prefer.)

3. Vertical spool pin with a felt pad under it; reduce the top tension slightly.
   Note: Sliver generally needs a lower top tension than Holoshimmer.

4. Outline stitch around the butterflies as desired. Add small stippling in open areas to make the butterflies pop, if desired.

Exercise 6: Square up the Pillow Top (Quilt Top)

You will need:
- 2 Quilt Rulers or a Drafting "L" Ruler • Rotary Cutter and Mat

1. Lay the quilted Pillow Top on a cutting mat. Line up one ruler with the bottom of the quilt, using the lines on the ruler so that one line lays along the seam line of the border. Put the other ruler vertically so it butts up against the first horizontal ruler and the edge of the quilt. Trim off excess batting and backing. Rotate the quilt and trim all sides so the "quilt sandwich" is square.

2. See page 46 for binding. Proudly hang your Sampler in your sewing room to display your first pieced and quilted wallhanging. Or see pages 51 to 59 for finishing as a pillow. *Congratulations!*

You could also feature computer embroidery!

If you own a computerized embroidery machine, another idea for this Pillow Top would be to feature your favorite 4" square designs.

Joyce Drexler's "Pressed Leaves" (43009GNP) by Great Notions has great home dec designs that look terrific on pillows and wallhangings. Or try Joyce's Fruit & Birds (43019GNP) by Great Notions for another seasonal look.

Find them at your favorite sewing store or on-line at: www.speedstitch.com.

We made our squares large enough to fit in the hoop and then trimmed them down to 6".

Binding the Quilt

*"We love well-made bindings. We are self-admitted binding snobs.
A lovingly applied binding is the finishing touch to a job well done!" - Beverly and Nancy*

Prepare the Quilt Top

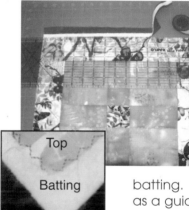

1. Prepare the quilt top for binding by trimming away the excess backing and batting. Use an inside seam as a guide to square up the quilt.

2. Choose a line that extends throughout the quilt. Line up the 6-1/2" x 24" ruler with that seam and determine how much to trim away.

3. Most measurements will be the size of the border less 1/4". Use the 12-1/2" square ruler to square the corners. Connect these cuts with the 6-1/2" x 24" ruler. A 60mm rotary cutter makes this job much easier.

Straight Grain Binding

1. Measure all four sides of the quilt and determine the total length of binding fabric required.

2. Cut the necessary number of crosswise grain strips, of the desired width (we suggest 2"), to equal the total length needed. Add an additional 36" to allow for seams and turns. Trim away selvages.

3. Piece these strips together diagonally, trim the seam allowance to 1/4", and press the seams open. Press the entire strip in half lengthwise.

4. Open up one end of the continuous binding and cut it at a 45° angle. Press under a 1/4" fold. Apply a 1/4" strip of Steam-a-Seam 2, fusible web tape, on the right side of the fold. Remove the release paper.

5. On the right side of the quilt, position the binding along the side of the quilt, 12" up from the bottom right hand corner. With the binding strip open, sew a scant 1/4" seam down about 6". Cut threads.

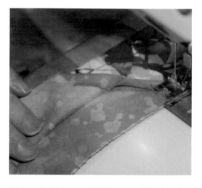

6. Then fold the strip lengthwise again. Both raw edges of the binding should be flush with the raw edge of the quilt top. Pin in place, if desired. Using the 1/4" foot, start sewing 6" from the diagonally folded end of the binding. Stop sewing a quarter inch from the edge of the quilt top. Backstitch.

7. Remove the quilt from the machine and clip your threads.

8. Flip the loose binding strip up and away from the quilt. Fold it back down, making sure the fold aligns with the edge of the quilt. Make

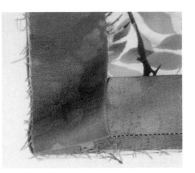

the turn along the next side and start sewing 1/4" in from both edges. There will be a loose triangle of fabric that will become your mitered corner after it is turned. Backstitch, being careful not to catch the loose triangle of fabric. See photo above.

9. Repeat for the remaining sides and corners.

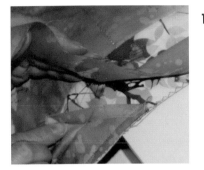

10. After finishing the last corner, sew up to 6" away from the beginning edge of the binding. Stop sewing with the needle down in the fabric.

11. Make sure that the binding ends overlap by at least 6".

12. Open the end of the binding so that it lays flat, wrong side up. Cut the binding at a 45° angle.

13. Lay the ending strip of the bind-

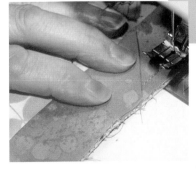

ing inside the beginning binding strip. The edge of the beginning binding will slightly extend over onto the batting. This is okay because it reduces bulk. Pin in place. Continue sewing until you overlap the beginning stitches. Backstitch. Clip threads and remove the quilt from the machine.

14. Place a strip of 1/4" Steam-a-Seam 2 on the back of the quilt along the cut edge. Remove the release paper and finger press. Turn the binding to the back of the quilt, making sure that the stitching

line does not show. Press. Hand stitch the binding in place with Sulky Poly Deco thread; fold the mitered corners neatly.

Back

Front

This Steam-A-Seam Tip is from Dianne Bungay, Canadian "Sew Exciting"™ Seminar Educator.

Bias Binding

It is the binding of choice for quilts in competition and it is essential to accommodate scalloped edges or curved corners. It is made the same way as straight grain binding, except the fabric is cut on a 45° (or bias) angle. Sew as instructed under Straight Grain Binding, or refer to continuous bias on page 60.

Binding Tips:

1. *Sulky Poly Deco™ Thread is wonderful for hand sewing bindings (as well as needle-turn applique) because it is fine but strong, and it flows through the quilt like butter.*

2. *Stripes and plaids cut on the bias are strikingly effective in jazzing up a quilt.*

3. *Never short-change a quilt by wrapping the backing over the edge to form a binding. It does not wear well.*

Make this quick & easy Quilted Scrappy Tablecloth for your favorite Holiday.

Measure your table's width and length to determine how many blocks you will need to make. We had a 38" x 60" table.

Fabrics & Supplies for Scrappy Holiday Tablecloth

All strips are cut across the fabric, selvage to selvage, assuming 42" of usable fabric. Use 1/4" seam allowance. Cut off all selvages. Yardage is figured for a 60" oval table allowing for a 5" overhang. Make a Fabric Key - see page 8.

- ❖ Fabric for patchwork - 1/8 yd. each of 11 fabrics
  From each, cut (1) 5" x 42" strip. Then cut strips in half on fold line to measure 5" x 21".
- ❖ Theme fabric for patchwork - 1-3/4 yds.
  Cut (10) 5" x 42" strips. Then cut strips in half on fold line to measure 5" x 21".
- ❖ Fabric for backing - 1-1/2 yds.
- ❖ Fabric for binding - 1/2 yd.
- ❖ Border - optional if you want a larger overhang
- ❖ Heat-resistant batting/fleece - at least 48" x 75"
- ❖ Sulky 12 wt. & 30 wt. Cotton Blendables™ Thread
  #4004 Golden Flame
- ❖ Machine needle: 14/90 Topstitch
- ❖ General sewing supplies - see page 3

Quick Scrappy Strip-Piecing Method

1. Sew (3) 5" x 21" strips together from the 11 fabrics as illustrated below, alternating the placement of the theme fabric. Press toward the theme fabric. Make 7 sets of each configuration.

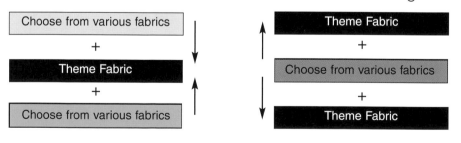

2. Using a rotary cutter, mat and ruler, cut into 5" strip sets.

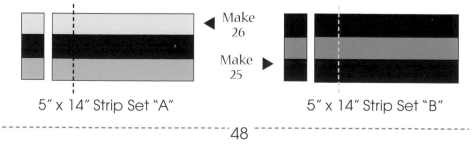

◀ Make 26

Make 25 ▶

5" x 14" Strip Set "A"   5" x 14" Strip Set "B"

Festive Holiday Throw Pillows
Joyce used the Beginner Sampler instructions on page 36 to make this pillow.

Tablecloth Finished Size: 53-1/2" x 72"

Credits: Level: Beginner - Good Starting Project
Tablecloth & Pillow by: Joyce Drexler
Leaf Theme Fabric by: Cranston for VIP

49

■ Assemble the Strip Sets into Blocks

1. Sew the strip sets together, matching seams. Make a total of (15) 9-patch blocks consisting of 3 strip sets with a different mix of coordinating fabrics that alternate with the theme fabric. Make 8 Block 1's and 7 Block 2's.

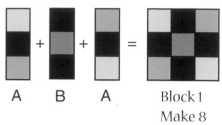 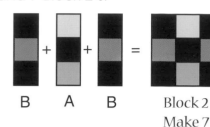

A   B   A   Block 1   B   A   B   Block 2
                Make 8   Make 7

2. Sew Block 1's and 2's together so that a theme fabric is always separating the mixed coordinating fabrics. (You could also make your patchwork tablecloth less scrappy by using just 2 different fabrics.)

••• Add borders if needed to achieve the length and width desired.

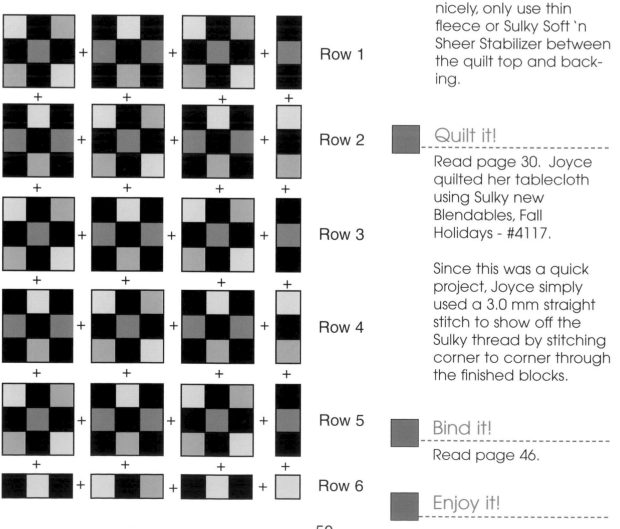

Row 1

Row 2

Row 3

Row 4

Row 5

Row 6

■ Add Borders •••
Read page 26.

■ Layer it!
Read page 28. Because you want your tablecloth to drape nicely, only use thin fleece or Sulky Soft 'n Sheer Stabilizer between the quilt top and backing.

■ Quilt it!
Read page 30. Joyce quilted her tablecloth using Sulky new Blendables, Fall Holidays - #4117.

Since this was a quick project, Joyce simply used a 3.0 mm straight stitch to show off the Sulky thread by stitching corner to corner through the finished blocks.

■ Bind it!
Read page 46.

■ Enjoy it!

Quick & Easy
Pillows & Cushions

Pillows add so much to any decor. Arrange them on a couch, toss them on a bench, use them on the patio swing or pile them high on a bed --- pillows add pizzazz anywhere you use them.

Pillows and cushions are a real home decoration that can be fabric coordinated either to your quilts and/or the table linens you use, to express your interests, or to help decorate for holidays. Pillow-making gives you tremendous freedom with fabrics. Because pillows are easy and relatively inexpensive to make, you can let your imagination burst with creativity.

On the following pages, we will cover the basics in pillow construction and then give you some great ideas on how to embellish your pillows. One of the pleasures of making pillows is that it takes just basic sewing skills. If you've done any sewing at all, you should be able to follow the instructions successfully. Making pillows is so satisfying because your project is completed quickly, and a pillow is the perfect palette to feature other crafts you enjoy as well.

Blendables™ *Pillows*

These simple, pieced, machine-embroidered pillows make great quick gifts. Or, make them for your own home as an accent on a bed or couch. Our samples were made using Joyce's new embroidery card, Abstract Florals, Signature Series #107 from Cactus Punch. Learn how to make these fun pillows and finish them with either cording, ruffles, knife edge, prairie points, or a flange edge.

Fabrics & Supplies Needed for Pillow

All strips are cut across the fabric, selvage to selvage, assuming 42" of usable fabric. Cut off all selvages. Measurements are for completing one pillow only.

- ❖ Fabric A - Center for embroidery - 12" x 14"
- ❖ Fabric B - Pillow fabric: 1 to 1-1/2 yds.
- ❖ Fabric C - Additional finishing fabric - 1/3 yd.
- ❖ 12" Pillow form
- ❖ Warm & Natural™ Batting - 12" x 14"
- ❖ Sulky 12 wt. & 30 wt. Cotton Blendables Thread: #4017 Lime Sherbet, #4030 Vintage Rose and #4025 Hydrangea
- ❖ Sulky Fabri-Solvy™ Stabilizer - 12" x 14"
- ❖ Sulky Soft 'n Sheer™ Stabilizer - 12" x 14"
- ❖ Sulky KK 2000 Temporary Spray Adhesive
- ❖ Cactus Punch Sig. Series #107 Embroidery Card
- ❖ Machine needle size: 14/90
- ❖ General sewing supplies - see page 3

Credits:

Level: Beginner
Pillows designed by:
  Joyce Drexler
Featured Fabric:
  Hoffman - *"At Home in the Woods"*
  by McKenna Ryan
Ink used on T-shirt: Tsukineko
Some text taken with
permission from the book:
  "America Sews with Sue
  Hausmann, book 31."
Embroidery Card: "Abstract Florals,
  Cactus Punch Sig. Series #107
  by Joyce Drexler
Photos:
  Chuck Humbert Imaging
  and Claudia Lopez
  Photography

Joyce Drexler and Sue Hausmann on the set of the PBS TV show "America Sews with Sue Hausmann" show how to make an embroidered pillow as well as how to paint a frame with fabric ink for a Blendables embroidery on a tee shirt. Look for this show on your local Public Broadcasting Station (PBS).

Create the Basic Pillow

1. Spray KK 2000 on the wrong side of a 9" x 11" fabric and smooth Sulky Fabri-Solvy onto it. Joyce chose a muted watercolor fabric for the background because the coloration is very subtle, thereby eliminating the starkness of a solid fabric.

2. Thread the top with Sulky 30 wt. Cotton Blendables according to the Cactus Punch Embroidery Card. Put Sulky Bobbin Thread in the bobbin. Stitch out the design.

3. Rinse the embroidery to remove the sta bilizer. Allow to dry. Press.

4. Trim the embroidered piece to 5-1/2" x 7-1/2".

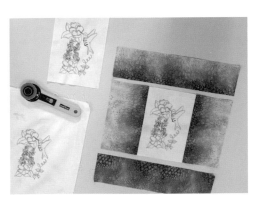

5. From a multi-colored fabric, cut (2) 4-1/4" x 7-1/2" border strips for the sides and (2) 3-1/2" x 13-1/2" strips for the top and bottom borders. (Joyce used a Hoffman fabric that was green and violet with lighter and darker sections. She "fussy-cut" the strips with the darker part on one edge and the lighter portion on the other.) Place the darker portion towards the center.

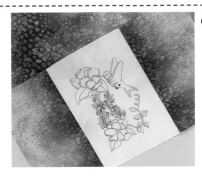

embroidered piece. Then stitch the top and bottom borders onto the block.

6. Use a clear 1/4" foot with a guide to stitch the side border pieces onto the 5-1/2" x 7-1/2"

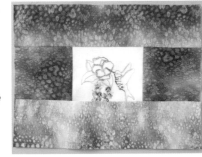

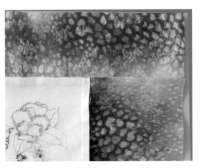

Press the seams toward the border fabric.

7. Lightly spray KK 2000 onto the wrong side of the pillow top and smooth it over a layer of cotton batting which is cut slightly larger than the pillow top. Spray KK 2000 onto a piece of Sulky Soft 'n Sheer which is cut as large as the batting; smooth the pillow top and batting layers over it, making a "quilt sandwich".

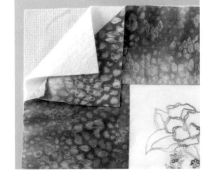

8. See page 30 and choose which quilting method best suits you. Once quilted, trim to pillow top size. See the next pages for the finishing styles.

Make a Slip-cover Back

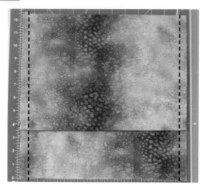

1. To finish your pillow, cut two 11" x 13" pieces for the back. On each piece, fold one of the 13" ends down 1" and press. Fold down another inch and press.

2. To secure the folds, topstitch close to both folded edges.

3. With the folded sides down, overlap the folded pieces to create a 13" square, and baste them together on both sides using a scant 1/2" seam allowance as indicated by the dotted lines above.

4. Place the finished pillow top onto the back, right sides together, and stitch all the way around using a 1/2" seam allowance. Turn right side out through the back opening. Press.

Insert a 12" Pillow Form

1. For sharp corners, stuff poly-fill into the corners before inserting the pillow.

Prairie Point Edge Finish

Make the basic pillow top as shown on pages 53 and 54.. Then use these instructions for finishing with a Prairie Point edge.

You will also need:

Note: Joyce chose a fabric with light and dark sections. If your pillow fabric choice offers this option, then from Fabric B:

❖ Cut (12) light 3-1/2" squares
❖ Cut (16) dark 3-1/2" squares

Make the Prairie Points

1. Fold all the squares diagonally and press.

2. Fold in half again and press.

Open

3. Place a dark point on each side of one corner of the pillow top. The side of the point with all raw edges should be aligned with the edge of the pillow top. The open side of the fold will always be to the left.

4. Tuck the points into each other between corners, alternating light and dark.

5. Points will measure approximately 1-1/2" apart from point to point. There are 7 Prairie Points per side. Pin one side in place and stitch 1/8" in from the edge of the pillow. Repeat for the other three sides.

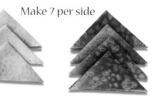

Make 7 per side

Flat Flange Edge Finish

Make the basic pillow top as shown on pages 53 and 54. Then use these instructions for finishing with a Flat Flange edge.

A "flange" is a flat, border-like edge, usually 2" to 4" deep, that frames a pillow top. It is usually cut as part of the top and bottom pieces, but can be pieced. The flange can match the pillow fabric or it can be seamed using two different fabrics. Flanged-edged pillows look best when the fabric has some body, such as in a high-count woven fabric. For a mitered flange, refer to mitered corners on page 27.

You will also need:

+ Cut (4) strips of Fabric B or C 2-1/2" x 42".
+ Cut both strips in half on the center bolt fold. You will now have (8) 2-1/2" x 21" pieces.

Make a Flanged Edge

1. Place the first strip on the top of the pillow top. Stitch. Trim the strip even with both ends of the pillow top.

2. Place the second strip on the bottom of the pillow top. Stitch and trim.

3. Place a strip on each side, stitching and trimming the same way.

4. Repeat for the back pillow piece. Make a Slipcover Back - see p. 54.

5. Place the pillow front and back, right sides together, and stitch around the pillow using a 1/2" seam. Turn through the back opening. Press.

6. Top stitch from the pillow front using Sulky 30 wt. Blendables; stitch in the seam thus creating the flange edge.

The quilting on this flange pillow is a grid style using a quilting guide on the foot. Draw one diagonal line with a chalk marker and then set up the guide attachment to help you keep the spacing uniform.

This pillow top using the Lakehouse Fabric has flanged borders that were not mitered. The pretty Floral Design is found on Sulky's website: www.sulky.com.

Welt/Piping Edge Finish

Make the basic pillow as shown on pages 53 and 54.
Then use these instructions for finishing
with a Welt/Piping edge.

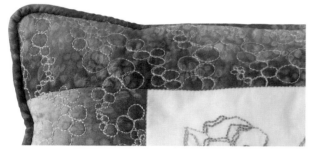

*Welt, sometimes referred to as "welting" or "piping",
is one of the most traditional edge finishes for
pillows, cushions and bolsters. Besides being
attractive, welt reinforces pillow seams and
helps keep edges straight.*

*At fabric, upholstery and quilting shops, you
can usually buy ready-made welting or piping (either
prepackaged or by the yard) that contrasts or
complements your pillow fabric, or you can make
your own welting using the following
general instructions.*

You will also need:

✦ Cut (2) strips on the bias
   1-1/2" x width of fabric
✦ 48" of 1/4" to 3/8" cording
✦ Zipper Foot or Cording Foot

How much welting is needed?

A knife-edge pillow needs a length of welting
(cord) equal to the pillow's finished perimeter
plus at least 3" for joining ends. For a boxed
cushion, you would double the perimeter
measurement and add 6".

Making your own welting or piping

Purchase plain "cord", sometimes referred to
as "cable cord", which comes in a wide
variety of diameters. For most pillows, a 1/4"
thick cord is perfect. For large floor pillows or
cushions, a much thicker welting will look

better. Many shops carry thick
cord for finishing off the edges on
bedspreads, tablecloths and large
pillows.

Cut your fabric on the bias to get
the best fit around the corners of
the pillow.

The fabric strip (referred to as the
casing) used to cover the welting
needs to be wide enough to wrap
around the cord, with enough extra
for twice the width of the seam
allowance, which is usually 1/2".
Refer to page 46 for instructions on
cutting continuous bias and for
joining strips.

1. Lay the cord along the center of
the wrong side of your casing.
Fold the casing over the cord,
matching up the raw edges.

2. Select a straight stitch with the
longest stitch length (basting)
and attach the zipper foot. Sew
through the casing close to the
cord (3/8" from the raw edge),
but not right next to it since you
will be stitching it to the pillow
top later and, at that time, you
will stitch between the welting
stitching and the cord.

Making Gathered Welting

Gathered or ruched welting gives a softer look. Instead of folding the casing over the cord and stitching, sew the casing to make a tube, and then feed the cord through it, gathering the casing. The best results are usually achieved by using a light to medium-weight fabric.

1. Tape the end of the cord to prevent fraying, then attach a small safety pin at the taped end. Thread the cord through the empty casing. Gather as you go and distribute the gathering evenly.

2. Pin the gathered welting to the pillow top, right sides together. Baste 1-1/2" from the end of the welting. Stitch the welting to within 1-1/2" of the corner. To turn the corner easily, make three or more diagonal cuts into the welt seam allowance, almost to the stitching. The simplest way to handle corners is to gently curve it around the corner. However, for square corners, continue stitching to within 1/2" of the corner; leave the needle down in the fabric; raise the presser foot; pivot the pillow top and welting; lower the foot; and stitch down the side.

Joining the Welting or Cord Ends

There are two ways to join the welting or cord ends:

1. *Fitting ends together:*
   Continue sewing around the pillow top, stopping (with the needle down) 1-1/2" away from the first welting end. With the needle in the fabric, cut off the second welt end so it will overlap the first end by 1 inch. Take out the last inch of stitching from the welt casing on the second end; pull the cord out and cut off one inch of cord. On this same end, fold the casing under 3/8" and lap it around the first end. Slip the cord back into the seam and hold it in place until you finish stitching the welting to the pillow top.

2. *Crossing ends:*
   Continue sewing around the pillow top until you get to within 1" of the first welting end. Stop stitching with the needle down in the fabric. Cut off the welting so it will overlap the first welting end by 1-1/2". Pull out and cut off 3/4" of cord from each end. With both ends extending into the seam allowance, cross the empty casing and finish stitching the welt to the pillow top.

Stitching Welted Pillow Together

With the welted pillow cover on top, make the final stitching between the welt stitching and the cord.

1. Since the pillow opening will be whip-stitched closed by hand, pin the pillow top and backing pieces with right sides together and raw edges aligned. Leave open most of one side of the pillow for inserting a pillow form later.

2. Using a 1/2" seam allowance, start stitching about 1-1/2" away from the lower corner on the open side, and end 1-1/2" beyond the other corner on the open side; clip the corners as you come

to them, and backstitch at the beginning and ending.

3. On the open side, press the seam allowances to make sharp, straight creases for easier hand stitching later.

Finishing the Pillow

1. Turn the pillow right side out. Press the edges if needed.

2. Insert a pillow form, working the corners of the form into the corners of the pillow. If the form doesn't completely fill the pillow corners, you may decide to add poly-fill in the corners.

3. Hand whip-stitch the opening closed.

Ruffle Finish

Make the basic pillow as shown on page 53. Then use these instructions for finishing with a Ruffle edge.

Ruffles are romantic. They soften whatever they are applied to... blouses, comforters, drapes, tablecloths and pillows. Adding two to three ruffles of different widths to a pillow just adds to its appeal. Also, combining ruffles with a contrasting welt in the seam can be dramatic. Sewing two strips of coordinating fabric together for a ruffle can create quite an impact as well.

You will also need:

- ❖ Edge Stitch Foot
- ❖ Ruffler Attachment (optional)
- ❖ Sulky 12 wt. Cotton

Make the 2 Ruffles - Option 1

1. To use a ruffler attachment to first stitch a double ruffle together and then apply it to the pillow top edge, start by cutting (3) 6" and (3) 8" strips across the full width of the fabric. Sew the narrow ends together to make 2 strips, each about 124" long.

2. Press in half lengthwise, wrong sides together. Place the narrower strip on top of the wider strip, matching the raw edges. Straight stitch along the raw edges to keep the layers together.

3. Attach your ruffler and set it for a 2 to 1 ratio. To test this setting, mark off and ruffle the first 10"; measure to see if it ruffled down to 5". If not, adjust the adjustment screw and retest until it is ruffling at a 2 to 1 ratio, then ruffle the strip to measure approximately 56" or more.

4. Place the ruffled strip on the edge of your pillow top with the raw edges aligned. Stitch the ruffle in place.

Make the 2 Ruffles - Option 2

Note: *We used contrasting colors of thread for photographic visibility. You should select a thread color that best matches the fabric you are using.*

1. Sew strips of one color fabric end-to-end into one long piece. Trim seams to a scant 1/4" and press OPEN. Fold in half lengthwise with wrong sides together. Press well. On each side of the folded fabric within the seam allowances, make chalk marks or place pins to indicate the 1/2 and 1/4 portions. These marks will help distribute fullness equally to matching portions on the pillow top.

2. Attach the edge stitch foot. Thread the top and bobbin with Sulky 12 wt. Cotton thread (or you can use 30 wt. in the bobbin). Because Sulky 12 wt. thread is very strong, it is ideal for gathering the ruffles.

3. Place the edges of the folded fabric under the edge stitch foot so that the raw edges are snug against the guide on the foot. Select a long, narrow zig-zag stitch. Hold a strand of Sulky 12 wt. Cotton in your hand and manually guide it under the foot while you zig-zag over it for the entire length of the piece The 12 wt. thread should lie freely under the zig-zag.

4. Pull up the 12 wt. drawstring thread until the circle of ruffles is the approximate size of the pillow top. Using the 1/2 and 1/4 marks as reference points, pin the narrow ruffle to the pillow top at those points. Ease the gathers so they are evenly distributed, and pin in place. Use your regular presser foot and stitch a straight stitch to the left of the previous zig-zag stitch to secure the ruffles. (You can baste this first and then straight stitch it if it makes it more manageable.)

No Finished Edge

Just seam the front to the back for a quick easy pillow finish. Below are more examples from Joyce's Blendables Cactus Punch Embroidery Card #107.

59

Box Style Cushions

Fabrics & Supplies Needed for Cushions

- ❖ Fabrics for cushions for a wrought iron chair -
  Measure chair to determine yardage needed.
- ❖ Fabric for bias welting - determined by
  measurement
- ❖ Zipper-by-the-yard - determined by your cushion size
- ❖ Foam - determined by measurement
- ❖ Brown craft paper on a roll
- ❖ Lining Fabric for light fabrics - Pam uses Dacron
- ❖ Triangle Ruler
- ❖ Sulky KK 2000 Temporary Spray Adhesive
- ❖ Magic Marker
- ❖ General sewing supplies - See page 3

Measure first, then cut

(Helpful hint: Be sure, when measuring the chair back, to allow
for the depth of the seat cushion.)

1. When making a box style cushion (such as the one on
   the next page) for a proper fit, first measure and then
   make a paper template of the chair seat and back.

2. Use Sulky KK 2000 to keep the template from shifting. If
   you are lining the cushion, you may also want to use
   KK 2000 to keep the
   lining and outer
   fabrics together.

3. Before cutting the
   fabric, cut out
   enough of the center
   of the template to
   see if the pattern on
   the fabric is centered
   on the chair seat and
   back.

4. If using the same
   fabric for both
   cushions, top and
   bottom, cut your
   cushion bottom in the
   same manner.

 Credits:

Level: Beginner
Box Cushions by:
  Pam Damour
Illustrations by:
  Katie Bartz
Photos by:
  Pam Damour
Featured Fabric:
  Lakehouse

Pam Damour

Make the Continuous Bias

"Continuous Bias" is a term
that refers to the technique
where fabric is sewn into a
tube, then cut in a spiral
fashion to create bias strips
in a very fast, efficient
manner. It requires no
more fabric than cutting
straight grain strips of
fabric but yields a strip
that has some "give" to it.

1. For the welting on this
   cushion, use the following steps to make 2"
   continuous bias. Begin
   with a square or
   rectangle of fabric
   that you have chosen
   to make bias welting.

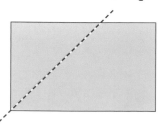

If you have porch furniture, then you know how hard it is to find cushions that both fit your chairs and match the rest of your decor. This project makes it easy. But if you want Pam and her team of professionals to make them for you, go to her website: www.pamdamour.com. The matching Table Topper Project is on page 87.

2. Use a triangle ruler to cut off a 45° angle from the fabric. Slide that triangle of fabric over to the other side and match the vertical edges.

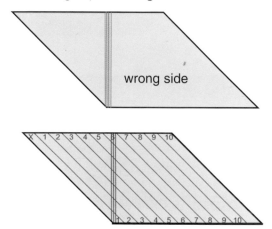

3. Turn the triangle over so the right sides are together, and sew the pieces together using a 1/2" seam allowance. Press the seam open, creating a parallelogram.

wrong side

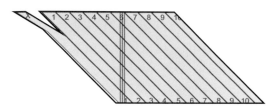

4. Draw lines on the wrong side of the fabric, the width of your desired bias (2") strips. Number your strips as illustrated.

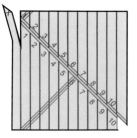

5. Cut about 2" in on the line between the "X" and #1.

6. Fold the fabric with right sides together; pin so that like-numbered strips are aligned, and stitch a 1/2" seam. Press all seams open and flat. Cut on the drawn lines to create an easy, uniform continuous bias strip.

7. To make welting, fold the 2" cut bias over 1/4" wide welt cord and stitch using a welting or zipper foot. To apply the welting to the cushion top, start at the center of the back edge of the cushion. Be aware that on a seat cushion, the back edge is at the top of the flowers (on this floral fabric), whereas on the back cushion, it is the stem edge of the flowers. (In our photo on page 61 we showed the reverse side of the cushion, green check.)

8. Clip the welting seam allowance at the corners as shown.

Splicing the Welting

1. Whenever there is a starting point and stopping point of the welting, it needs to be "spliced". To create a seamless splice, trim the starting end at a 45° angle and trim the overlapping welting straight across, leaving approximately a 2" overlap.

2. Unstitch the blunt-cut welting about 2-1/2". Laying the welt cords together, trim the blunt-cut welt cord at a 45° angle to match the other cord.

3. Fold remaining fabric under and wrap it around the welting. Finish sewing in place.

The Rise

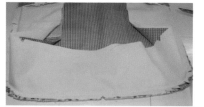

1. When making a cushion, the height of the cushion is referred to as the rise. The zipper on a box-style cushion requires some extra length to travel a few inches around a corner as well as the entire back edge. Be sure to allow about 8" of extra fabric all the way around for ease in the rise.

2. Cut the rise 1" deeper than the thickness of the cushion foam. For the zipper placket, cut two rises, each the depth of the front rise. For a standard rectangular cushion, the zipper portion of the rise should be the entire back of the cushion, plus travel around two corners. Allow 4" to 6" for each end of the zipper in addition to the back of the cushion.

3. Fold the rise in half lengthwise with wrong sides together. Sew in the zipper-by-the-yard with the folded edge close to the zipper teeth as shown. To provide ease in removing the cushion form without tearing the zipper, allow the zipper to turn the corner at each end and travel down the cushion sides at least 2" on each side.

4. Separate the zipper a couple of inches and insert the slide in the center of the zipper. Sew the "closed" end of the zipper, with right sides together and raw edges even to the other section of the rise.

5. Start at the center front of the cushion (matching any pattern in the fabric) and sew the rise to the cushion top all the way to the corner. Snip the rise 1/2" at the corner and turn the corner. Continue sewing halfway down the side. Sew the other side of the front in the same manner. Repeat for the back of the cushion, starting at the center back. Where the front and back rises meet at the sides, leave an excess of a few inches and fold over to create ease. This will make it much easier when sewing to the

other side of the cushion. The excess you've allowed will also create a "pocket" for the zipper slide to hide in, and give you a very professional finish.

6. After applying the rise to one side of the cushion, notch the opposite side of each corner of the rise to make your alignment markings for the other side. Sew the other cushion piece to the rise. Sew all the way around the cushion and

serge the seam allowances to finish. Open the zipper and turn right side out. Insert the cushion form.

Throw Pillows by Pam

It's always fun to make interesting pillows to complement your cushions, especially if you have nice rattan or wooden porch furnishings. Pictured above are some that Pam made from leftover fabrics from the cushions.

Check out pages 53-59 for steps on different finishes for pillows.

Look for Pam's and Katie Bartz's book on making cushions and pillows (to the right) and Pam's DVD, "The Decorating Diva", at your favorite fabric or quilt shop, or shop online at: www.pamdamour.com

Blendables™ T-shirt

Make a quick gift for someone special!
This project is ideal to do with the grandkids too!
It's fun! fast! and easy!

Supplies Needed for Blendables T-shirt

- ✤ Pre-washed white T-shirt (no fabric softener)
- ✤ Sulky 30 wt. Blendables™ Cotton
    Threads: #4017 Lime Sherbet, #4030
    Vintage Rose and #4025 Hydrangea
- ✤ Cactus Punch Signature Series #107
    Embroidery Card by Joyce Drexler
- ✤ Sulky Totally Stable™ Iron-on Stabilizer -
    5" x 7" and 12" x 15" pieces
- ✤ Sulky Fabri-Solvy Water Soluble Stabilizer -
    12" x 16" piece for embroidery
- ✤ Sulky KK 2000 Temporary Spray Adhesive
- ✤ Machine needle size: 14/90
- ✤ Tsukineko Inks: #11 Lemon Yellow
                     #22 Spring Green
                     #19 Cerulean Blue
                     #16 Peony Purple
                     #98 Vintage Wine
- ✤ Fabric pens - optional
- ✤ Paper towels
- ✤ 3-4 small bowls and a tub to hold them
- ✤ (3-4) 3" paint brushes and an eye dropper
    or liner brush
- ✤ General sewing supplies - page 3

Credits:

Level: Beginner
T-shirt designed by: Joyce Drexler
Ink used on T-shirt: Tsukineko
Embroidery Card: Cactus Punch
    Signature Series #107
    Abstract Florals

Paint and Embroider

1. Measure and pour 1/2 capful of both Peony Purple and Vintage Wine Tsukineko Inks in a small bowl. Stir.

2. Measure and pour 1/2 capful of both Lemon Yellow and Spring Green in another small bowl. Stir.

3. Pour 1/2 capful of Cerulean Blue into a third small bowl.

4. Add a capful of water to each bowl to make the ink a little lighter in color. Stir.

5. Dip a dry 3" brush into the Purple and Wine mixture. To prevent dripping onto the shirt, hold a paper towel under the brush as you take it to the T-shirt.

6. Lightly run the brush around and over all the edges of the 5" x 7" Totally Stable, with most of the ink being applied to the T-shirt.

Prepare the T-shirt for Painting

1. Place the T-shirt over the end of the ironing board so only the front of the shirt is on the board. Slide a 12" x 15" piece of Sulky Totally Stable under the shirt, shiny side up; center it 4" down from the neckline. Iron it in place.

2. Center the 5" x 7" piece of Totally Stable on top of the right side of the T-shirt, about 4" down from the neckline. Iron it in place.

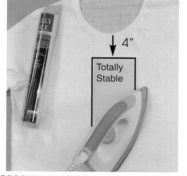

Remove the Totally Stable Stabilizer

7. Peel up and remove the Totally Stable from the front of the shirt.

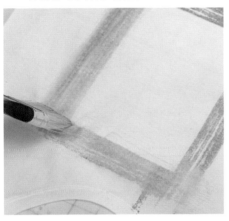

8. Dip another dry 3" brush into the Lemon Yellow and Spring Green mixture and lightly brush over the frame area. To prevent dripping onto the shirt, hold a paper towel under the brush as you take it to the T-shirt.

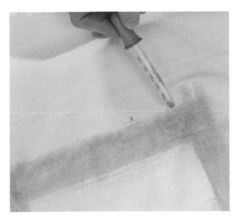

9. Using the eye-dropper, dot some blue in different areas of your choice over the frame.

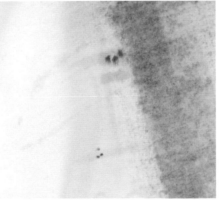

10. Using the eye-dropper or liner brush, add more horizontal lines with colors of your choice.

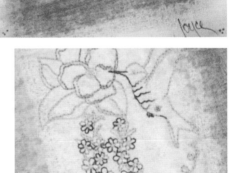

11. Iron dry to set the ink. Remove the Totally Stable and back the shirt with a 12" x 16" piece of Fabri-Solvy; embroider an Abstract Floral Design onto it, inside the frame.

Whole Cloth Quilting

Classy Vest from Upholstery Fabric embellished and quilted with Sulky Holoshimmer™ by Patti Lee.

Photos by: Chuck Humbert Imaging

Reversible Vest from Hand-Dyed Fabric by "Free Spirit", embellished and quilted by Evelyn Byler with Sulky Holoshimmer™ Metallic Thread.

Joyce Drexler on the left *(wearing a ready-made jacket that was quilted by Evelyn Byler using Sulky Blendable 12 wt. Cotton Thread)* and Karen Good *(wearing a jacket made from the Free-Spirit™ Color Flash collection by Heidi Stoll-Weber, quilted with a decorative stitch pattern using a Sulky Blendable 12 wt. Cotton)* on the set of the PBS TV Show, "America Quilts Creatively".

Joyce showed how easy it is to create your own personalized quilted cloth. She shared many friend's vests and jackets made from a single fabric that had been embellished and quilted using a variety of Sulky Decorative Threads and Stabilizers. Joyce is holding a vest by Ellen Osten that was made from Drapery Fabric.

Join in the fun of using those special fabrics you have been saving for just the right project--- this is it! Wear it, display it, or use it in your home for a decorative project. The perfect palette for your favorite free-motion quilting techniques! See page 33 for instructions on free-motion quilting.

Fabrics & Supplies Needed:

Cut off all selvages before cutting out a pattern.

✤ Enough yardage of your favorite
  fabric for the project you have chosen
✤ Sulky Decorative Threads
✤ Warm and Natural™ Fleece
✤ Sulky Soft 'n Sheer & Solvy Stabilizers
✤ Sulky KK 2000 Temporary Spray Adhesive
✤ General Sewing Supplies - see page 3

Credits:

Level: Beginner
Whole Cloth Quilted Clothing designed by:
Evelyn Byler, Joyce Drexler, Patti Lee,
and Ellen Osten
Quilt quilted by: Evelyn Byler

*Make your own quilted cloth for ---
Clothing, Pillows, Tablecloths,
Placemats, etc.*

Whole cloth quilting begins with a single fabric. We all buy fabrics with no particular project in mind just because we love the color, texture or design of a print. We keep it in the closet and get it out once in a while to look at it and admire it... *but we don't dare cut it!*

This is the fabric that is ideal for whole cloth quilting. Sometimes, you will want to embellish all over it with Sulky decorative thread, or just add Sulky Thread to certain areas to enhance the design. But mostly, you will want to quilt it.

The beautiful throw to the right is a prime example. I simply loved this fabric --- just the way it was. Because I couldn't bear to cut it up, I gave it to my friend, Evelyn Byler, and asked her to use her long-arm quilting machine to simply quilt it as one piece.

Refer to page 28 for layering a quilt. Often for clothing I will use Sulky Soft 'n Sheer, a permanent stabilizer, instead of batting between the backing and top because it helps to stabilize the fabric for decorative stitching while keeping the garment lightweight and cool. Of course, I use Sulky KK 2000 to keep the layers together while stitching.

Refer to pages 12-15.
If you live in a warm climate but want
to be able to wear a vest year-round, try this
fool-proof method for stabilizing your yardage
for decorative stitching and quilting.

Close-up of a ready-made Barn Jacket
embellished with Sulky Blendables #4033.
by Joyce Drexler

What's old is new again!
Get an old jacket out of the closet
and texturize it for a brand new look.
Joyce used an all-over design.
Open up the sleeves and work on them flat.
Stiffen the jacket with a water-soluble
stabilizer solution to make stitching a breeze!

If using a washable fabric:
In a plastic tub, bucket or sink, dissolve
(2) 20" x 36" pieces of water soluble Sulky
Solvy™, or half that much Super Solvy™, in
16 oz. of water. Mix until all the Solvy is dissolved. Place your yardage in the solution until all of the fabric is saturated.
Hang until almost dry. Iron the fabric dry.
It will now be stiff so you will be able to
stitch it without worrying about puckering
or distortion.

Once embellished, rinse out the stabilizer.
If using a paper pattern to cut out a garment, spray the wrong side of the paper
lightly with Sulky KK 2000 and smooth the
paper pattern onto the fabric. NO PINS
NEEDED! Cut out the pattern pieces.
Remove the pattern and construct the
garment.

If using a non-washable fabric:
Lightly spray Sulky KK 2000 on the wrong
side of the fabric and smooth Sulky Soft
'n Sheer Permanent Stabilizer over it. The
stabilizer will keep the decorative stitching from puckering or tunneling and it
can serve as the fleece layer when quilting.

If making either a whole cloth placemat, pillow top, cushion or tablerunner,
the same principles can be applied.

Quilted Fiber Bubbles Jacket

Credits:

Level:
Intermediate
Jacket by:
Diane Gloystein
National Sulky
Educator
Fabrics: Silk
Dupioni and
Organza
Pattern used:
Vogue 7714
Photos by:
David Dale
Photography
Lincoln, NE

Fish Bag Pattern:
Linda McGhee
www.ghees.com

This project uses elastic thread in the bobbin. Since different fabrics will react differently to the introduction of elastic thread, you will need to experiment.

Also, different machines will react differently to elastic thread in the bobbin. You may need to decrease your bobbin tension and increase the top tension. Your fabric will shrink about two times its orginal size once it has been shirred.

Inserted
Bubbles

Trim Insert in
Jacket Front

Lining of Jacket

Fabrics & Supplies - Jacket Insert

- ✤ Your favorite Jacket pattern (Diane used Vogue 7714)
- ✤ Free-motion foot   ✤ Serger - optional
- ✤ Machine needle: 14/90 Topstitch
- ✤ Sulky 30 wt. Cotton or Rayon Thread and Sulky Holoshimmer Metallic Thread
- ✤ 2-Toned Silk Dupioni - the amount your pattern suggests
- ✤ 15" x 45" piece of Silk Dupioni for panel
- ✤ 1" x 1-1/2" assorted rectangles of organza in various colors
- ✤ Sulky KK 2000 Temp. Spray Adhesive
- ✤ Sulky Solvy™ Water Soluble Stabilizer
- ✤ Sulky Cut-Away Plus™ Stabilizer
- ✤ 6 yds. of piping   ✤ Elastic Thread
- ✤ 6" wooden machine embroidery hoop
- ✤ General sewing supplies - see page 3

Note: Diane's instructions are to make a panel inset that you can customize to any size for insertion in your jacket.

Step 1

1. Spray Sulky KK 2000 Temporary Spray Adhesive on the right side of your 15" x 45" Silk Dupioni.

Step 2

1. Arrange a variety of different colored 1" x 1-1/2" organza rectangles on top of your 15" x 45" piece, randomly overlapping them. Diane did "Fiber Bubbles" on about 8" of the 15" width. Her completed "Fiber Bubble" strips are about 3" wide. Cover the arranged fabric rectangles with a layer of Sulky Solvy. Hoop into a 6" wooden machine embroidery hoop.

Step 3

1. Set up your machine for free-motion. See page 33.
2. Thread a coordinating color of Sulky 30 wt. Cotton Thread through the 14/90 topstitch needle.
3. Slowly wind the elastic thread onto the bobbin. Insert the bobbin into the bobbin case.
4. Bring the elastic thread to the top of the fabric. Stitch in place for 3-4 stitches to secure your threads. Clip threads. Try stitching both with the thread in the tension and with it by-passing the tension to see which works best to make the fabric draw up and crinkle (shirring).
5. Straight stitch overlapping circles about the size of a quarter. The circles do not need to be identical.

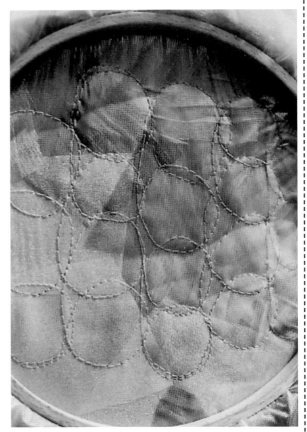

6. Keep in mind that much of the shirring occurs when you take it out of the hoop and steam the completed piece. Play with the tensions on a small test piece until you are satisfied with the shirring.

Step 4

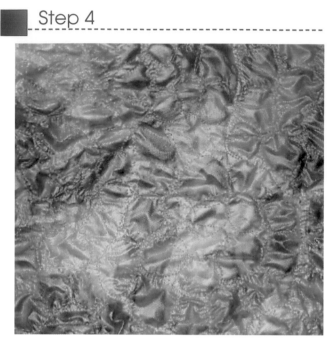

1. Remove the hoop and put another layer of organza rectangles on top of your Silk Dupioni, directly below the area that you have just shirred.

2. Cover with a layer of Solvy. (Flatten out your fabric prior to hooping to avoid any tucks in your fabric.) Hoop and repeat the process of stitching overlapping circles as in Step 3.

Step 5

1. Repeatedly follow the directions in Step 4 until the entire surface (or as much as you desire) of Silk Dupioni has been free-motion stitched; then remove the Solvy by placing the fabric in a lingerie bag and washing it in your washer without detergents or softeners.

2. Dry the fabric in the dryer on the delicate setting.

Step 6

1. Now that the Solvy has been removed, hold the iron just above your shirred, organza-covered piece. Steam. Do not touch the iron to the fabric because organza can melt.

Step 7

1. Lay the completed, "bubbly", shirred fabric on a similar size piece of Cut-Away Plus and baste the shirred fabric to it. The Cut-Away Plus stabilizes the bumpy, textured piece, giving you a firmer, more manageable piece. The Cut-Away Plus can be cut away once the piece is inserted into the jacket.

2. Do not try to stretch your shirred piece flat. On the back of the Cut-Away Plus, mark the width that you want the finished shirred piece to be; serge, or use an overcast stitch, on this line. Insert your shirred piece into your garment or applique area. Cut away the stabilizer.

☐ Credits:

Level: Beginner - Easy
Quilt designed & pieced
  by: Beverly Morris
Quilted by: Abigayle's
  using Sulky 100% Cotton
  30 wt. White Thread
Featured Fabric: Flannel

Try this alternative look, using a striped fabric for the binding. Beverly loved the candy cane effect the striped fabric created.

She also wanted a color-block effect so she made each individual 9-patch block from the same flannel print and color.

☐ Credits:

Quilt pattern by:
  Beverly Morris
Designed by:
  Joyce Drexler
Pieced by:
  Nancy Sapin
Quilted by: Sue Moats
  using Sulky Blendables
  Cotton Thread #4102.

Featured Fabric:
  Frederick Warne & Co.
  and Benartex Minkee.

Quilt it using Sulky 100% Cotton Blendables Thread. The rapidly changing colors will make even your very first quilt one of interest and beauty.

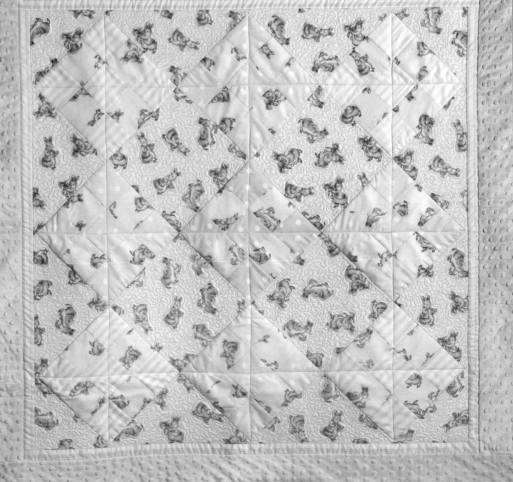

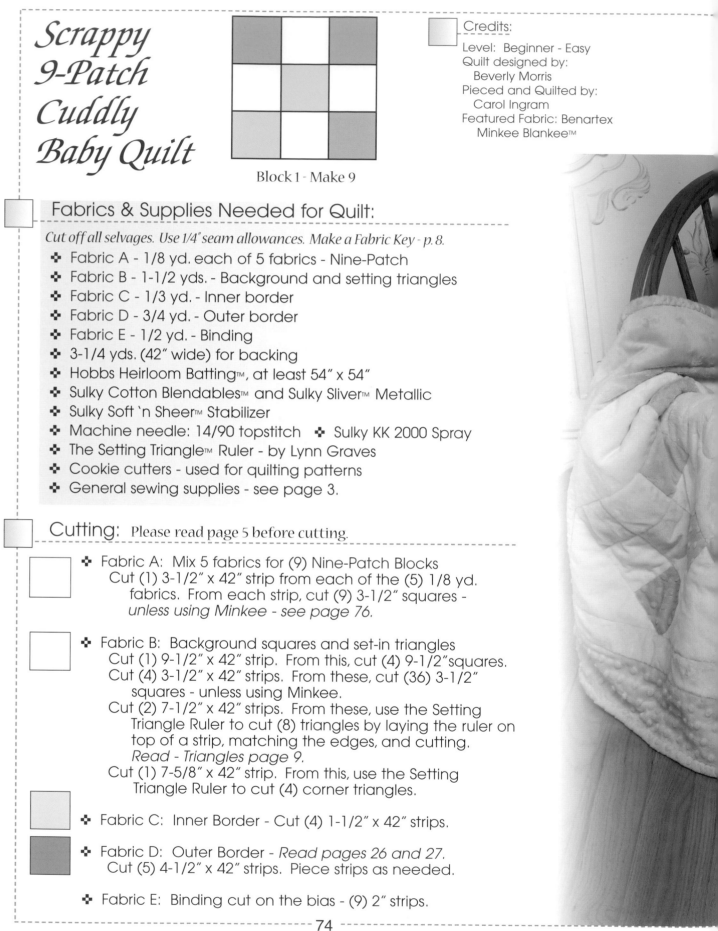

Scrappy 9-Patch Cuddly Baby Quilt

Block 1 - Make 9

Credits:
Level: Beginner - Easy
Quilt designed by:
  Beverly Morris
Pieced and Quilted by:
  Carol Ingram
Featured Fabric: Benartex
  Minkee Blankee™

Fabrics & Supplies Needed for Quilt:

Cut off all selvages. Use 1/4" seam allowances. Make a Fabric Key - p. 8.

❖ Fabric A - 1/8 yd. each of 5 fabrics - Nine-Patch
❖ Fabric B - 1-1/2 yds. - Background and setting triangles
❖ Fabric C - 1/3 yd. - Inner border
❖ Fabric D - 3/4 yd. - Outer border
❖ Fabric E - 1/2 yd. - Binding
❖ 3-1/4 yds. (42" wide) for backing
❖ Hobbs Heirloom Batting™, at least 54" x 54"
❖ Sulky Cotton Blendables™ and Sulky Sliver™ Metallic
❖ Sulky Soft 'n Sheer™ Stabilizer
❖ Machine needle: 14/90 topstitch ❖ Sulky KK 2000 Spray
❖ The Setting Triangle™ Ruler - by Lynn Graves
❖ Cookie cutters - used for quilting patterns
❖ General sewing supplies - see page 3.

Cutting: Please read page 5 before cutting.

❖ Fabric A: Mix 5 fabrics for (9) Nine-Patch Blocks
  Cut (1) 3-1/2" x 42" strip from each of the (5) 1/8 yd.
  fabrics. From each strip, cut (9) 3-1/2" squares -
  unless using Minkee - see page 76.

❖ Fabric B: Background squares and set-in triangles
  Cut (1) 9-1/2" x 42" strip. From this, cut (4) 9-1/2" squares.
  Cut (4) 3-1/2" x 42" strips. From these, cut (36) 3-1/2"
  squares - unless using Minkee.
  Cut (2) 7-1/2" x 42" strips. From these, use the Setting
  Triangle Ruler to cut (8) triangles by laying the ruler on
  top of a strip, matching the edges, and cutting.
  Read - Triangles page 9.
  Cut (1) 7-5/8" x 42" strip. From this, use the Setting
  Triangle Ruler to cut (4) corner triangles.

❖ Fabric C: Inner Border - Cut (4) 1-1/2" x 42" strips.

❖ Fabric D: Outer Border - *Read pages 26 and 27.*
  Cut (5) 4-1/2" x 42" strips. Piece strips as needed.

❖ Fabric E: Binding cut on the bias - (9) 2" strips.

Another Baby Project by Carol Ingram
✤ Baby Moses Basket - See page 79.

Quilt Size: Approx. Finished Size 50" x 50"
See other fabric versions on page 73.

Make 9 Patch Blocks — *If using Minkee Blankee fabric, read the tip below.*

1. Use a 1/4" seam allowance throughout. Sew a 3-1/2" fabric "A" square to both sides of a 3-1/2" fabric "B" square. Make 9. Repeat to make 9 of a second 3-block strip. Then, sew one fabric "B" square to both sides of a fabric "A" square. Make 9.

2. Press seams toward the darker squares as indicated by the arrows.

3. Sew the patchwork strips together to form a 9-patch block. You can keep colors in the same position as you make the 9 blocks, or move them around as desired.

■ + □ + ■ = [ ][ ][ ] Make 9

□ + ■ + □ = [ ][ ][ ] Make 9

□ + □ + ■ = [ ][ ][ ] Make 9

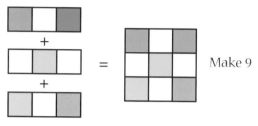

Make 9

Carol's Tip: Flip and Sew Method if using Minkee

Since you cannot press the seams of Minkee without pressing out the little raised dots, designer Carol Ingram has developed the technique below to sew Minkee together without pressing the seams or having the fabric curl, slip or roll.

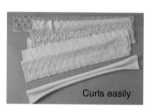

Curls easily

Soft'nSheer

Soft'nSheer

1. Cut (5) 3-1/2" x 42" strips of your selected Minkee colors, and (4) 3-1/2" x 42" strips of the background color.
2. Cut (4) 10" x 42" strips of Sulky Soft 'n Sheer.
3. Spray Sulky KK 2000 Temporary Spray Adhesive on the wrong side of (1) 3-1/2" x 42" strip of Minkee; smooth it evenly onto the outside edge of the 10" x 42" strip of Soft 'n Sheer.
4. Alternating background and color strips, lay a second 3-1/2" x 42" strip of Minkee, right sides together, over the first strip and stitch the inside seam through the Soft 'n Sheer Stabilizer.
5. Spray KK 2000 on the wrong side of the second strip, fold it over and smooth it evenly onto the Soft 'n Sheer. The KK 2000 and Soft 'n Sheer act as a substitute for pressing and they make it easier to seam Minkee together without slipping.
6. Lay the third strip, right sides together, over strip 2; stitch together.
7. Spray KK 2000 on the wrong side of the third strip, fold it over and smooth it onto the Soft 'n Sheer.

Make 4 Sets: 2 with background fabric on both outside strips and one color strip on the inside (center); 2 with the background fabric as the inside (center) and 2 color strips on the outside. (Do not cut away the stabilizer.) Cut them into 3-1/2" strips and sew them together (butting seams) into (9) 9-Patch Blocks.

For best results, spray all other Minkee pieces with KK 2000 and smooth them onto Soft 'n Sheer before cutting and sewing. Mix up the colored strips for a scrappy effect, making all the blocks slightly different.

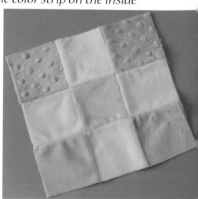

Using The Setting Triangle™ Ruler

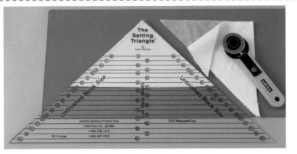

This must-have ruler will become your best quilting friend. It will take all the math and guesswork out of cutting setting triangles.

Read page 10 and the ruler insert for complete instructions.

Sew 9-Patch Blocks to Background Squares and Setting Triangles

1. Using a 1/4" seam allowance, sew together, in the 5 rows as indicated below, the (8) background fabric triangles, the (4) 9-1/2" squares, and the (9) 9-Patch Blocks. Do not sew the (4) corner triangles yet. Press seams toward background fabrics.

2. Sew a corner triangle to each corner. Use a 12-1/2" square ruler to trim the corners. Line it up against the quilt top so the fabric edges will be cut 1/2" away from the outermost point of the 9-Patch Block. Use a 6-1/2" x 24" ruler to connect the cuts along the sides. Now the top is perfectly square!

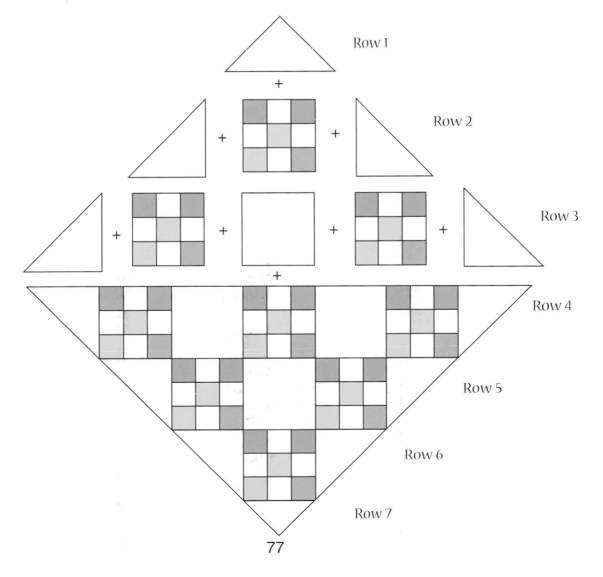

Add Inner Border Strips "Fabric C" - *see page 26 for measuring tips*

1. Measure and cut inner border strips according to the directions on page 26. Then sew the inner border strips to the left and right sides. Press seam allowances toward the inner border strips.
2. Repeat for the top and bottom inner borders. Press toward the inner border strips.

Outer Borders

Use the 4-1/2" strips of Fabric D. *Read pages 26 and 27.*

Layering & Quilting

Read pages 28 - 30.

Binding *Read page 46.*

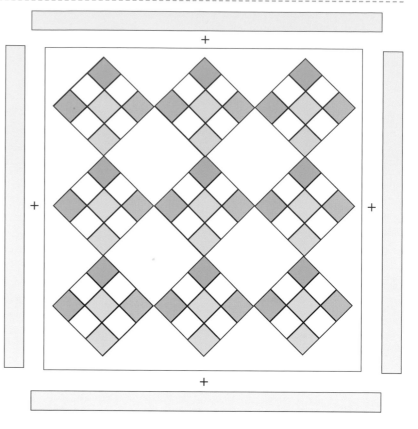

Carol had so much fun making this soft and cozy scrappy quilt using different colors and textures of Minkee™ Fabric.

She also used a multi-format software program called 3-D Sketch™ by Husqvarna to embroider the cute animal cookie cutter designs.

78

Moses Basket

Credits:
Level: Beginner Designed by: Carol Ingram
Chenille Fabric: Benartex

Fabrics & Supplies Needed for Moses Basket:

*All strips are cut across the fabric, selvage to selvage,
assuming 42" of usable fabric. Cut off all selvages.*

- (1) 33" woven, oval, rope-handled basket
- 2" mattress foam, cut to shape of bottom of the basket
- 1 yd. pre-quilted plain fabric
- 3 yds. solid, coordinated to theme fabric
- 4 yds. of eyelet ruffle
- 1-1/2 yds. of 3/4" wide elastic
- 3 yds. 1" wide matching satin ribbon (optional)
- 3-1/4 yds. 1/2" wide matching satin ribbon
- Sewing thread to match project
- Walking foot or even-feed foot
- Sulky KK 2000 Temporary Spray Adhesive
- General sewing supplies - page 3
- 3 yds. nursery theme fabric
- 2 pieces of cotton batting 7" x 33"
- 4 yds. cording (optional)
- Air soluble marker

Step 1: Cover the Mattress

1. Double the pre-quilted fabric and lay the mattress foam on it. With an air soluble marker, draw around the mattress, adding 1/2" for the seam allowance. Cut out both layers of fabric on the drawn lines; also cut out a paper pattern this size (possibly from newspaper) to use later in the project.

2. For the sides of the mattress cover, cut a strip of the pre-quilted fabric 3" wide by the length all around the perimeter of the mattress.

3. Using a 1/2" seam allowance, serge or sew the right side of the 3" strip to the right side, all around, of the first mattress bottom. Serge the right side of the other mattress bottom to the right side of this strip, leaving an 8" opening for turning.

4. Turn right side out, insert the mattress into the cover and hand stitch the opening closed.

Step 2: Measure the Basket

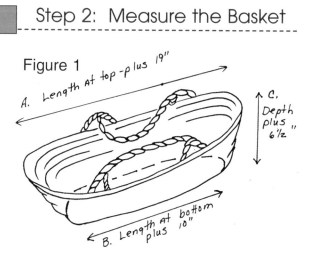

Figure 1

1. Measure the outside basket length across the top center (A), figure 1, and add 19".

2. Measure the length across the outside bottom center (B) and add 10".

3. Measure the depth (C) and add 6-1/2".

4. Measure the handle opening from the outside of one rope edge to the outside of the other rope edge.

5. To measure for the sheets, lay the covered mattress on a piece of paper and draw a line around it, 3-1/2" away from the edge of the mattress to allow for the sheet to be turned under. Cut out the pattern.

6. Using this paper pattern, cut two sheets from the same or different fabric.

Step 3: Cut the Fabric

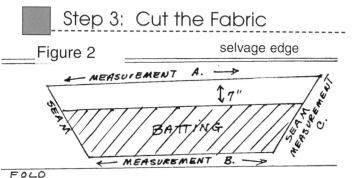

Figure 2

1. Double the printed fabric lengthwise, as in Figure 2 above.

2. Using the basket cover measurements as determined in Step 2 (with added amounts), draw lines marking top (A), bottom (B), and height (C). Cut out.

3. Use the same measurements to cut out the solid lining fabric.

4. Cut a strip of cotton batting to the proper angle and length for placement at the lower edge of the basket as indicated in Figure 2.

5. Cut two bottoms, one printed and one solid, from the newspaper pattern that you cut out in "Cover the Mattress" - step one. With both right sides facing out, serge or sew them together around the outside edge using a 1/2" seam allowance.

80

Step 4: Construction

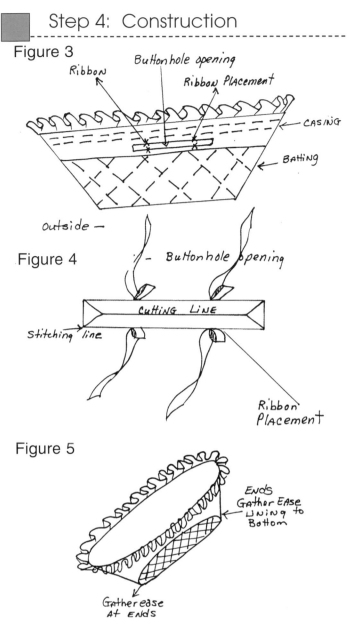

Figure 3

Ribbon
Buttonhole opening
Ribbon Placement
CASING
BATTING
outside —

Figure 4

Buttonhole opening
Cutting Line
stitching line
Ribbon Placement

Figure 5

Ends
Gather Ease
Lining to
Bottom
Gather ease
at ends

1. With the right sides of both the printed fabric and plain fabric together, sew a seam across the ends. Turn and press.

2. Sew cording to the eyelet ruffle (if desired). Then sew the ruffle to the top right side of the printed piece.

3. With the right sides together and the ruffle turned down, sew the lining and outside together at the top, along the ruffle. Turn, press and smooth in place.

4. Lay the project on a table, right sides out, straighten, open to inside and place batting between the lining and the outside in proper placement as indicated in Figure 2. Use Sulky KK 2000, smoothing and spreading the layers as you go.

5. Attach a walking foot or even-feed foot and put Sulky 40 wt. Rayon Thread on the top and in the bobbin. Sew cross-hatch quilting lines over the entire area about 4" apart, through all layers (where the batting lays) to hold them in place (Figure 3).

6. Create a casing for the elastic by sewing two lines of straight stitching below the ruffle (Figure 3); put the first line 1-1/2" from the ruffle and the second line 1-1/4" from the first line.

7. Pin the prepared bottom piece to the bottom of the prepared basket lining, matching ends; gather, easing fullness as you pin. Serge into place.

8. Place the partially finished lining in the basket and smooth it into place. Insert the covered mattress inside and smooth the sides over the edge of the basket to get the handle placement. With an air soluble marker, mark where the rope handles are attached. This indicates placement for "buttonhole" opening, (Figure 3).

Step 5: Buttonhole Opening

With this step you are going to effectively make a large bound buttonhole with ties on the sides.

1. Remove the lining from the basket.

2. On the outside of the prepared basket lining, use an air soluble marker to draw a straight line indicating where the

outside handle placement would be (Figure 4).

3. Draw a 1" wide rectangle around this line, keeping the line centered in the middle of the rectangle. Mark corner triangles as indicated in Figure 4.

4. Cut two pieces of accent fabric 2" wide by the length of the drawn rectangle, plus 2".

5. Center one of these 2" wide strips over your drawn rectangle for the opening. Pin. Stitch around outside line. Cut open on the cutting line and clip into the corners. Roll and turn to the inside. Hand stitch down to create a finished opening. Repeat for the other side.

6. Cut the 1/2" wide ribbon into 8 equal pieces, approximately 14" each. On each side of the buttonhole opening, loop one end of ribbon under itself about 1" and sew it in place as indicated in Figure 4 for the tie closures. Repeat for the other side.

Step 6: Elastic Casing

1. At one end of the casing at the top of the basket lining, clip a few stitches so you can insert the elastic.

2. Using a very large safety pin (or bodkin) attached to the end of a strip of elastic, thread enough elastic through the casing until you get the desired fullness in the gathers to stretch over the edge of the basket. Clip and sew the ends of the elastic together. Pull and stretch the elastic until it is in place inside of the casing, and it is gathered evenly.

3. Place the lining in the basket. Stretch the elastic over the edge of the basket, and the buttonhole openings over the handles. Use the ribbon to tie it all securely in place.

Step 7: Finishing

Sew 1/4" elastic around the edges of the serged sheets by either using an elastic foot or by stretching the elastic while zig-zag stitching along the elastic. Stretch it over the mattress. Place the mattress inside the basket.

Les Fleurs Placemats

Invite the girls to a "Sew and Sleep-over Party".
Each of you make a placemat to use the next morning
for a delightful breakfast of tea,
French pastries and berries!

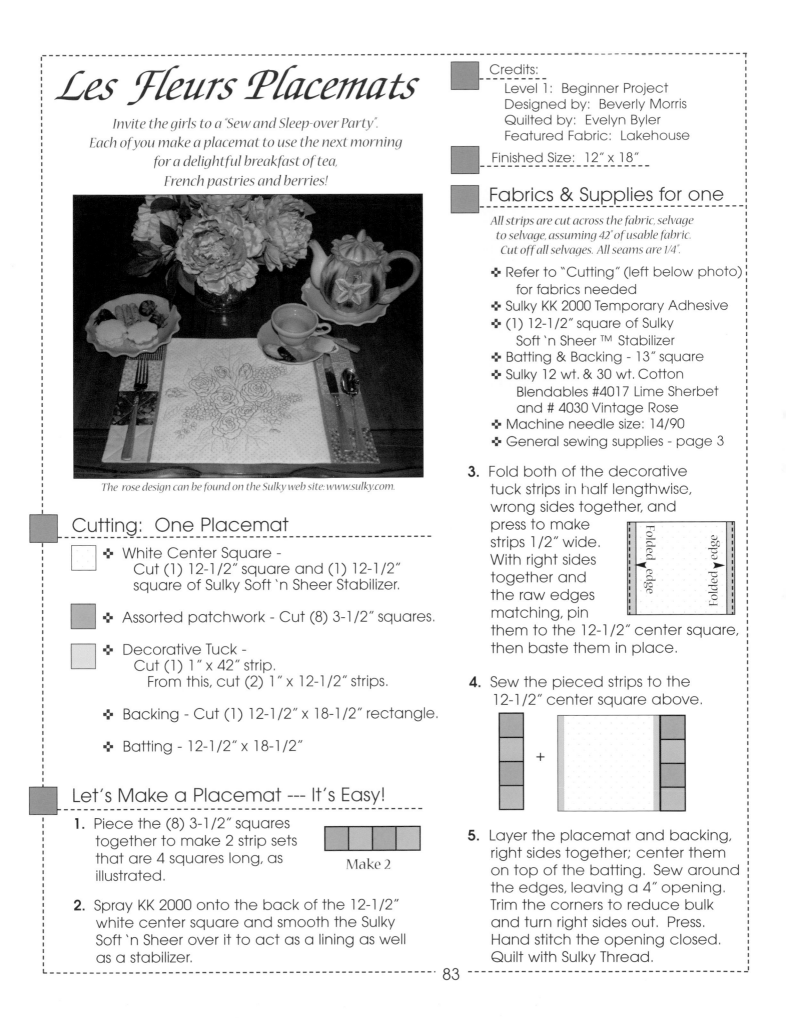

The rose design can be found on the Sulky web site: www.sulky.com.

Credits:
Level 1: Beginner Project
Designed by: Beverly Morris
Quilted by: Evelyn Byler
Featured Fabric: Lakehouse

Finished Size: 12" x 18"

Fabrics & Supplies for one

All strips are cut across the fabric, selvage
to selvage, assuming 42" of usable fabric.
Cut off all selvages. All seams are 1/4".

❖ Refer to "Cutting" (left below photo)
   for fabrics needed
❖ Sulky KK 2000 Temporary Adhesive
❖ (1) 12-1/2" square of Sulky
   Soft 'n Sheer ™ Stabilizer
❖ Batting & Backing - 13" square
❖ Sulky 12 wt. & 30 wt. Cotton
   Blendables #4017 Lime Sherbet
   and # 4030 Vintage Rose
❖ Machine needle size: 14/90
❖ General sewing supplies - page 3

Cutting: One Placemat

❖ White Center Square -
   Cut (1) 12-1/2" square and (1) 12-1/2"
   square of Sulky Soft 'n Sheer Stabilizer.

❖ Assorted patchwork - Cut (8) 3-1/2" squares.

❖ Decorative Tuck -
   Cut (1) 1" x 42" strip.
      From this, cut (2) 1" x 12-1/2" strips.

❖ Backing - Cut (1) 12-1/2" x 18-1/2" rectangle.

❖ Batting - 12-1/2" x 18-1/2"

Let's Make a Placemat --- It's Easy!

1. Piece the (8) 3-1/2" squares
   together to make 2 strip sets
   that are 4 squares long, as
   illustrated.

   Make 2

2. Spray KK 2000 onto the back of the 12-1/2"
   white center square and smooth the Sulky
   Soft 'n Sheer over it to act as a lining as well
   as a stabilizer.

3. Fold both of the decorative
   tuck strips in half lengthwise,
   wrong sides together, and
   press to make
   strips 1/2" wide.
   With right sides
   together and
   the raw edges
   matching, pin
   them to the 12-1/2" center square,
   then baste them in place.

   Folded edge   Folded edge

4. Sew the pieced strips to the
   12-1/2" center square above.

   +

5. Layer the placemat and backing,
   right sides together; center them
   on top of the batting. Sew around
   the edges, leaving a 4" opening.
   Trim the corners to reduce bulk
   and turn right sides out. Press.
   Hand stitch the opening closed.
   Quilt with Sulky Thread.

Les Grand Fleurs

Jaunty rows of flowers quickly grow into a delightful, quick and easy quilt. Easy piecing of multi-colored squares make the alternate rows fast and fun to put together. Raising a beautiful garden has never been so trouble free!

Feature a border or striped focal print. Choose a pleasing balance of the repeated border design you wish to showcase.

Credits:
Level: Beginner Quilt - Easy
Designed by: Beverly Morris
              and Joyce Drexle
Quilted by: Evelyn Byler
Featured Fabric: Lakehouse
As seen on the "Fons & Porter" PBS TV Quilting Show.

Fabrics & Supplies Needed for Quilt:

All strips are cut across the fabric, selvage to selvage, assuming 42-1/2" of usable fabric. Cut off all selvages. Amounts required will be determined by the border print chosen. All seams are 1/4".

- ❖ Approx. 3/4 yd. of a floral print or 3 repeats of a 6-1/2" border print
- ❖ 1/4 yd. each of 11 complementary fabrics
- ❖ 3/4 yd. for bias binding
- ❖ Approx. 2 yds. (42" wide) for backing
- ❖ Hobbs Heirloom Batting - at least 46" x 70"
- ❖ Sulky 12 wt. & 30 wt. Cotton Blendables™
- ❖ Machine needle size: 14/90
- ❖ General sewing supplies - see page 3

Cutting: Make a Fabric Key - page 8. Read page 5 before cutting.

- ❖ Large Floral Print - Cut (3) 6-1/2" x 42-1/2" strips.

- ❖ Scrappy Patchwork - Cut (2) 3-1/2" x 42-1/2" strips from each of 11 fabrics. Then cut these strips in half making the strips 3-1/2" x 21-1/4".

- ❖ Pink Accent - Cut (2) 2" x 42-1/2" strips. Cut (1) 3-1/2" x 42" strip.

- ❖ Green Dot - Cut (3) 2" x 42-1/2" strips.

- ❖ Pink & Green Stripe - Cut (1) 2" x 42-1/2" strip. Cut (2) 3-1/2" x 42-1/2" strips.

Quick & Easy Home Decorating Projects:
  • Pillows • Square Table Topper • Knitting Bag • Placemats

Quilt Finished Size: Approx. 42-1/2" x 66-1/2"

See other fabric versions on pages 87, 89, and 91.

Create Pieced Units -1/4" seams

Tip: Sew the blocks together in small sections of 4 or 6. The shorter seams will provide greater accuracy. Press to the dark when it is possible, but don't hesitate to press the seam again in order to reduce bulk and nest the seam.

1. Using a stitch length of 2mm and scattering the colors, sew together the 3-1/2" x 21" strips into sets of 2. Press seams toward the darker fabric.

2. Cut these sets into (70) 3-1/2" wide 2-patch sets.

3. Randomly sew together these 2-patch sets to make a Unit 1 and a Unit 3, which are each 2 squares by 14 squares.

Unit 1 and Unit 3

4. Sew together the 2-patch sets from step 2 above into units of 6 squares. Then sew these into a Unit 2 and a Unit 4, which are each 3 squares by 14 squares. You will have blocks left over due to the "scrappy" piecing process. Press seams to one side.

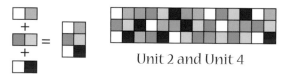

Unit 2 and Unit 4

Assemble the Units

1. Sew these patchwork units to the border prints, adding as many additional coordinated fabric strips as illustrated below to achieve the desired length.

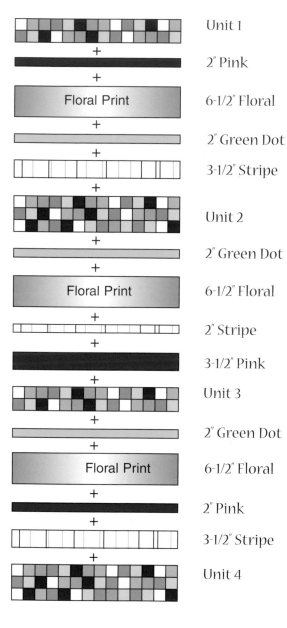

Unit 1
+
2" Pink
+
6-1/2" Floral
+
2" Green Dot
+
3-1/2" Stripe
+
Unit 2
+
2" Green Dot
+
6-1/2" Floral
+
2" Stripe
+
3-1/2" Pink
+
Unit 3
+
2" Green Dot
+
6-1/2" Floral
+
2" Pink
+
3-1/2" Stripe
+
Unit 4

Finishing the Wallhanging

See pages 28 - 37 for layering, quilting and binding.

Apple Time   Try using any theme fabric instead of florals!

Credits: Beginner - Easy Patchwork   Quilt designed by: Joyce Drexler   Pieced by: Patti Lee and Carol Ingram.   Quilted and free-motion embroidered by: Evelyn Byler using Sulky 40 wt. Rayon Thread for thread enhancement of the fabric apple theme print; Sulky Holoshimmer Metallic #6055 Cranberry in the ditches; Sulky 30 wt. Cotton Blendables to stipple the theme print and Sulky 12 wt. Cotton Blendables over the patchwork squares.   Featured Apple Fabric: Michael Miller

Refer to piecing
directions on
pages 84 - 86.

This could be the
perfect quilt
for your next picnic
in the park.

Below:
Apple Time
Table Topper.
See page 92
for complete
instructions
for making one
for your
kitchen table!

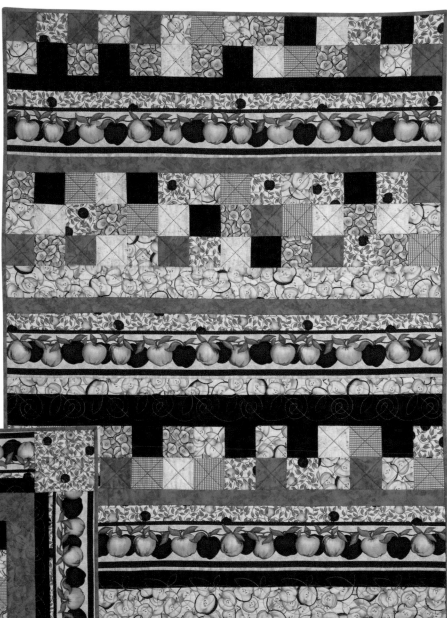

Quilt Finished Size: 42-1/2" x 66-1/2".

Les Grand Fleurs Embroidered Wallhanging

Nothing could be as lovely as creating a garden of beautifully embroidered cut flowers using Sulky 40 wt. Rayon, Sulky Totally Stable and Sulky Tear-Easy Stabilizers. A great quilt for featuring your 5" x 7" embroidered flowers from Joyce's Grand Flower Collection.

Fabrics & Supplies for Embroidered Version:

All strips are cut across the fabric, selvage to selvage, assuming 42-1/2" of usable fabric. Cut off all selvages.

❖ Refer to page 84 for fabric amounts and cutting
❖ "Grand Flowers Collection #1", #43021 GNP by Joyce Drexler for Great Notions
❖ Embroidered Flowers - Sulky 40 wt. Rayon listed on card
❖ Sulky Totally Stable™, and 2 layers of Sulky Tear-Easy™ or 1 layer of Sulky Stiffy™
❖ Quilted with Sulky 12 wt. Cotton Blendables #4001 Parchment and #4106 Primaries; and Sulky Sliver Metallic #8040 Opalescent for stitching in the ditch
❖ Machine needle: 14/90 Embroidery
❖ General sewing supplies - see page 3

Embroider the Flower Strips: (We used 3 strips.)

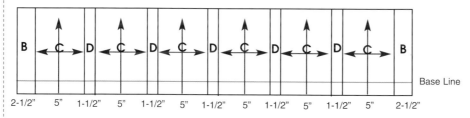

Base Line

2-1/2" 5" 1-1/2" 5" 1-1/2" 5" 1-1/2" 5" 1-1/2" 5" 1-1/2" 5" 2-1/2"

1. For the 3 embroidered strips, cut (3) 10-1/2" x 42-1/2" strips.

2. Iron a 10-1/2" x 42-1/2" strip of Sulky Totally Stable Stabilizer onto the wrong side of the fabric.

3. Allow to cool, then use a wash-out or air-soluble marker to mark the right side of the fabric strip as follows:
   A. Base line --- 2-1/2" up from the bottom of the strip.
   B. Draw a line 2-1/2" in from each end, creating space B.
   C. On each end, draw another line 5" over from B. This is the space C where the first 5" x 7" embroidery will be.
   D. On each end, draw another line 1-1/2" over from the 5" space C. This marks the space D between the embroideries.

Continue repeating C & D until the 42-1/2" strip is completed.

4. To make a template for placement of each flower embroidery, put a horizontal and vertical mark on the strip to indicate the beginning point of each embroidery. Since each flower may vary in size, be sure that the bottom of the flower will always rest on the base line.

5. Spray Sulky KK 2000 onto 2 additional layers of Sulky Tear-Easy Stabilizer (or 1 layer of Sulky Stiffy) to hold them together and adhere them to the Totally Stable.

6. Start on the left side of the strip and embroider the first flower.

7. Continue until all flowers are embroidered, then carefully remove the stabilizer and sew the strip to the patchwork.

Follow construction instructions on page 86 except substitute a continuous "Embroidered Flower" strip for large flower fabric print strips. Note patchwork placement. You can choose how long you want your quilt to be by either adding additional coordinated fabric strips of varying widths and/or small black sashing strips to finish each patchwork segment.

You can also change the height of the embroidered background fabric strips. (Ours were 10-1/2".)

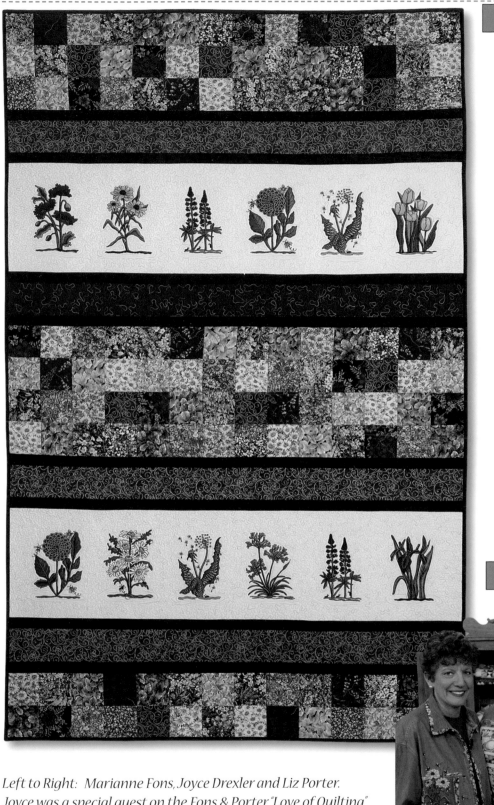

Credits:

Level: Beginner patchwork and *easy embroidery by machine*

Wallhanging designed and pieced by: Joyce Drexler

Quilted by: Evelyn Byler using Sulky Sliver Metallic #8040 Opalescent in the ditches only, Sulky 12 wt. Cotton Blendables #4001 Parchment stippled around the embroideries, and Sulky 12 wt. Cotton Blendables #4106 Primaries stitched over patchwork.

Featured Fabric: Mostly Robert Kaufmann small florals and swirls.

Featured Embroidery: "Grand Flowers Collection #1", #43021 GNP by Joyce Drexler for Great Notions.

Finished size: 42-1/2" x 66-1/2"

Left to Right: Marianne Fons, Joyce Drexler and Liz Porter. Joyce was a special guest on the Fons & Porter "Love of Quilting" PBS TV Show - Series 800, that showcased all the Grand Fleur Quilts that appear in this book. She showed the use of fabric border prints, the computer embroidered borders featured above, as well as how to place and stabilize designs to achieve the best results.

Les Grand Fleurs
Embroidered & Inked

It's fun to use embroidered thread sketches (redwork designs)
stitched either by hand, free-motion or computer embroidered as motifs to color
with crayons, fabric paints or inks!

Follow construction instructions on page 86, except substitute a continuous-embroidered flower strip for fabric printed flower strips. Refer to the photo on the next page for patchwork and embroidery placement.

Fabrics & Supplies for Painted Version:

Refer to page 84 for fabric amounts, cutting and piecing
- 1-1/4 yd. White Dyer's Cloth - 100% Cotton
- Embroidery machine with a 5" x 7" hoop
- Grand Flowers Embroidery Card #43021 GNP, 28 outline only designs by Joyce Drexler for Great Notions ®
- Thread for Flowers - Sulky 30 wt. Cotton #1005 Black
- Sulky Stabilizers - Solvy 1 yd. package and Totally Stable on 12" Roll
- Quilted with Sulky Blendables #4003 Sunset and Holoshimmer Metallic Thread #6032 Lime
- Machine needle size: 14/90
- General sewing supplies - see page 3

Supplies for Painting:

- Tsukineko Fabric Pens and Inks
- Paper Towels & Water
- Small-Tipped Soft Paint Brush
- 2" Soft Paint Brush
- Small cups for mixing
- Eyedropper

Prepare fabric for Embroidering:

Cut (3) 15" x 42-1/2" fabric strips from white Dyer's Cloth cotton fabric. Soak them in a Sulky Solvy solution (20" x 36" piece of Solvy to 8 oz. of water). Allow to dry. Press. Refer to page 88 for laying out embroideries. Each strip will have 6 flowers stitched onto it. Allow 5" per flower with 1-1/2" between each. Mark for positioning of flowers. Embroider the outline only, as directed. With the embroideries centered, trim the fabric strips to 10-1/2" x 42-1/2".

Ink the Embroidered Flower Strips:

1. After the flowers are embroidered, wash out the Solvy. Allow to dry. Press. Iron Sulky Totally Stable Stabilizer onto the wrong side.
2. In a spray bottle or bowl, mix 6 oz. of water with the ink until you have the color you wish the background to be. (Joyce chose a yellow/orange mixture.) The ink will dry lighter than the mixture looks.
3. Spray plain water on the embroidered fabric strip to slightly dampen it. Spray the ink on an unembroidered piece for practice, or use a small paint brush to apply the ink mixture, and adjust the mixture as desired. Then, spray so the ink frames the embroidered flowers. If desired, use an eyedropper to add droplets of the orange ink sparingly.
4. Choose a palette of ink and permanent fabric pen colors that complement the fabric patchwork.
5. Color in the flowers as desired. On our sample, Joyce put a light wash of colors first and then, using the pens, added stronger color for accent.

Credits: Level 1: Beginner Wallhanging designed and inked by: Joyce Drexler

Quilted by: Evelyn Byler using Sulky 12 wt. Cotton Blendables #4003 Sunset, and Sulky
       Holoshimmer™ Metallic #6032 Lime Green to stitch in the ditches.

Embroidery: "Grand Flowers Collection #1", #43021 GNP by Joyce Drexler for Great Notions -
       Outlines Only using Sulky 30 wt. Cotton #1005 Black.

Inks: Tsukineko Fabric Pens and Inks

Featured Fabric: Clothworks - "Flying Colors" - Laurel Burch

Finished Size using only 2 patchwork sections: 42-1/2" x 53"

Les Fleurs Table Topper

*Continue the adventure into Spring.
In just a few hours time you can
assemble a delightfully French country
table topper to match your wallhanging!*

Credits:
Level 1: Beginner Project
Designed by: Beverly Morris
Quilted by: Evelyn Byler
Featured Fabric: Lakehouse

Finished Size: 34-1/2" square

Cutting:

❖ Large Floral Print -
Cut (4) 5-1/2" x 21-1/2" strips.

❖ Scrappy Patchwork -
Cut (25) 3-1/2" squares
from 6 - 8 different fabrics.

❖ Striped Border -
Decide which direction
works best for cutting
the stripes.
Cut (4) 3-1/2" x 42" strips.
From these, cut (2) 3-1/2"
x 15-1/2" and (2) 3-1/2" x
21-1/2" strips.

❖ Green Inner Border -
Cut (2) 2" x 43" strips.
From these, cut
(4) 2" x 21-1/2" strips.

❖ Corner Blocks -
Cut (4) 7" squares.

Fabrics & Supplies for Table Topper

*All strips are cut across the fabric, selvage to selvage,
assuming 43" of usable fabric. Cut off all selvages.
Amounts required will be determined by the border
print chosen. All seams are 1/4".*

❖ Approx. 3/4 yds. of a repeating border print
❖ 1/4 yd. each of 6 - 8 complementary fabrics
❖ 1/2 yd. for bias binding
❖ Approx. 1 yd. for backing
❖ Hobbs Heirloom Batting, approx. 38" square
❖ Sulky 12 wt. & 30 wt. Cotton Blendables™
❖ Machine needle size: 14/90
❖ General sewing supplies - see page 3

Assemble the Table Topper

1. Sew (25) 3-1/2"
squares into a
25-piece
square,
alternating
colors. Press
seams in the
direction of the
arrows.

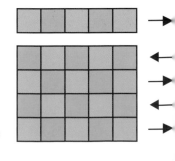

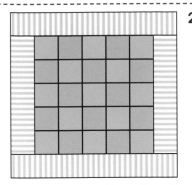

2. As illustrated, sew the (2) 2-1/2" x 15-1/2" striped borders to the 2 sides; then sew the (2) 3-1/2" x 21-1/2" striped borders to the top and bottom. Press seams in the direction of the striped inner border fabric.

3. Sew the (4) 2" x 21-1/2" inner borders to the tops of the (4) 5-1/2" x 21-1/2" floral print borders. Press toward the inner border.

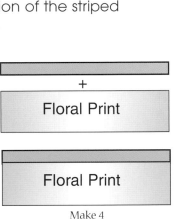

+

Floral Print

Floral Print

Make 4

4. Sew two of the floral print/inner border strip sets to opposite ends of the table topper center. Press toward the striped border.

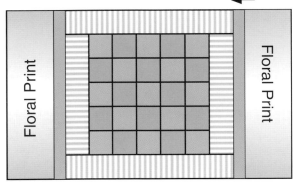

Floral Print

Floral Print

5. Sew the 7" corner squares to each end of the remaining (2) strip sets.

Floral Print

6. Sew these strips to the top and bottom of the table topper.

Floral Print

Floral Print

Floral Print

Floral Print

Tablerunner

Finished size: 12" x 30"

Cutting and Finishing

Cut (3) 6-1/2" center squares.
Cut (28) 3-1/2" squares, or use scraps.
Cut Backing Fabric and Hobbs Heirloom Batting 15" x 36".

1. Sew (2) 3-1/2" squares together. Make 6 sets. Attach one set to the top and bottom of each 6-1/2" center square.

2. Sew (4) 3-1/2" squares together. Make 4 sets. Attach one set to each side of the center square sets.

3. To finish, see #5 on Page 83.

On-the-go Knitting Bag

Fabrics & Supplies Needed for Bag

All strips are cut across the fabric, selvage to selvage, assuming 42" of usable fabric. Cut off all selvages.

- ❖ Cut (3) 4-1/2" x 26" strips of coordinating fabrics.
- ❖ Cut (2) 5" x 11" strips of coordinating fabrics for the sides of the bag.
- ❖ Cut (2) 12-1/2" x 18" strips of an accent fabric for the inside pocket.
- ❖ Cut (2) 5" x 11" pieces of fusible batting.
- ❖ Cut (1) 12-1/2" x 18" piece of Sulky Cut-Away Plus Stabilizer for the pocket lining.
- ❖ Cut (2) 2" x 21" strips of Sulky Cut-Away Plus Stabilizer to line the handles.
- ❖ Cut (1) 4" x 42" strip of any coordinate for handles. Cut in half to make strips that measure 4" x 21".
- ❖ Cut (1) 1" x 4-1/2" strip for button loop.
- ❖ Cut (1) 12-1/2" x 26" piece of fusible batting for the strip set.
- ❖ Cut (1) 12-1/2" x 26" piece of a lining fabric.
- ❖ Sulky 30 wt. Cotton Thread   ❖ Sulky KK 2000
- ❖ (1) 1-1/2" decorative button
- ❖ Machine needle size: 14/90 Topstitch
- ❖ General sewing supplies - see page 3

Credits:

Level: Beginner - Easy
Knitting Bag designed by:
  Nancy Bryant
Featured Fabric: Lakehouse
Finished Size: 15-1/2" wide
  (including sides) x 12-1/2"
  deep x 4" bottom

Let's Begin

1. Sew the (3) 4-1/2" x 26" strips of coordinating fabrics into a strip set.

12-1/2" ⟶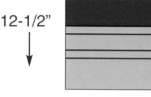

2. Press the 12-1/2" x 26" fusible batting onto the back.
3. Put Sulky 30 wt. Cotton Thread on the top and in the bobbin. Use a 14/90 topstitch needle and embellish seams with decorative stitches through all layers.
4. Press the (2) 5" x 11" pieces of fusible batting onto the back of the (2) 5" x 11" fabric pieces for the sides of the bag.
5. Mark the center of the longest side of each of the 12-1/2" x 26" strip sets on both sides.
6. Mark the center of the 5" side of each of the 5" x 11" pieces.
7. Place the 5" x 11" piece, right sides together, with the 12-1/2" x 26" strip set, matching the center marks.

8. Make a mark 1/4" from the beginning and end of the 5" side of the 5" x 11" side pieces.
9. Start sewing 1/4" from the beginning of the 5" x 11" side piece and stop 1/4" from the end. Backtack at the end of this seam.
10. Pivot the end panel, aligning the raw edges of both pieces. Pin in place.

Using a 1/4" seam allowance, stitch up one side, starting from the 1/4" mark and continuing to the top of the bag. Repeat with the other 5" x 11" piece to complete the sides.

Lining

1. Layer the pocket fabrics, right sides together, and place the Sulky Cut-Away Plus Stabilizer on top.
2. Stitch the top and bottom seams, leaving the sides open.
3. Turn the pocket right side out. Press.
4. Mark the center of the width of the pocket at both ends.
5. Mark the center of the length of the lining at both sides.
6. Place the pocket on top of the 12-1/2" x 26" lining fabric, with the raw edges matching the center points.

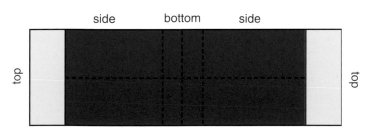

7. Stitch across the center horizontally, back-stitching at each end to make two equal pockets.
8. Stitch down the center vertically, and then 2-1/4" away from each side of the center seam to form the bottom.
9. Add side rectangles as in steps 6-10 of the outside section.

Handles

1. Fold each 4" x 21" strap in half lengthwise. Press. Place the Sulky Cut-Away Plus Stabilizer inside the strap, snug against the fold. Spray with KK 2000 to hold it in place.
2. Fold edges inside to make the straps measure 2" wide. Press flat.
3. Topstitch along both edges to reinforce the strap.

Button Loop

1. Fold the 1" x 4-1/2" strip in half lengthwise to measure 1/2" x 4-1/2"; press.
2. Fold in both short sides 1/4" each so that the strip measures 1/2" x 4"; press.
3. Fold in each long raw edge a scant 1/4" up to the fold so that the strip measures 1/4" x 4"; press.
4. Topstitch along the folded, open edges the length of the loop to reinforce it.

Assemble the Bag

1. Place the handles 1" from each side of the top edge of the bag. Position each handle, raw edges together, on the outside of the bag. Baste in place.
2. Place the loop in the center of the bag, raw edges together and positioned on the outside of the bag. Baste in place.
3. Turn the bag right side out. Slip the bag inside the lining, which is wrong side out.
4. Make sure the handles and button loop are pushed down, out of the way; line up raw edges. Pin.
5. Stitch around the top of the bag, leaving a 3" opening to turn the bag right side out.
6. Turn the bag, hand-stitch the opening closed, and press. Topstitch around the top of the bag.
7. Sew a large decorative button in place. Grab your knitting and enjoy!

Marine Biology

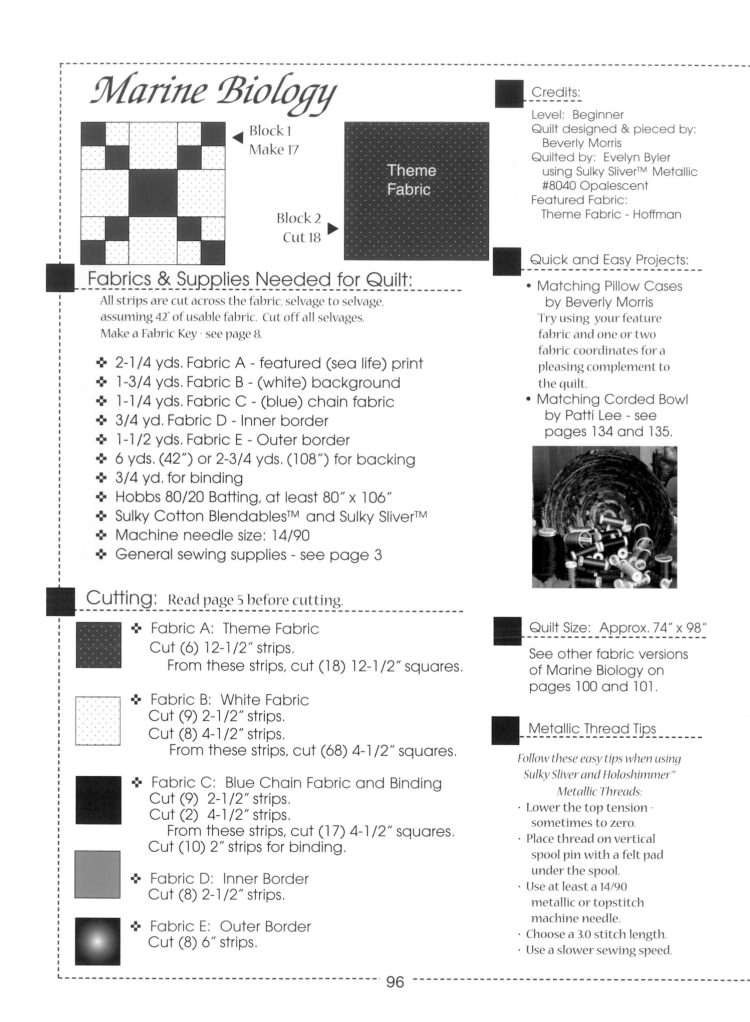

◄ Block 1
Make 17

Block 2 ►
Cut 18

Theme
Fabric

Credits:
Level: Beginner
Quilt designed & pieced by:
  Beverly Morris
Quilted by: Evelyn Byler
  using Sulky Sliver™ Metallic
  #8040 Opalescent
Featured Fabric:
  Theme Fabric - Hoffman

Fabrics & Supplies Needed for Quilt:

All strips are cut across the fabric, selvage to selvage,
assuming 42" of usable fabric. Cut off all selvages.
Make a Fabric Key - see page 8.

- ❖ 2-1/4 yds. Fabric A - featured (sea life) print
- ❖ 1-3/4 yds. Fabric B - (white) background
- ❖ 1-1/4 yds. Fabric C - (blue) chain fabric
- ❖ 3/4 yd. Fabric D - Inner border
- ❖ 1-1/2 yds. Fabric E - Outer border
- ❖ 6 yds. (42") or 2-3/4 yds. (108") for backing
- ❖ 3/4 yd. for binding
- ❖ Hobbs 80/20 Batting, at least 80" x 106"
- ❖ Sulky Cotton Blendables™ and Sulky Sliver™
- ❖ Machine needle size: 14/90
- ❖ General sewing supplies - see page 3

Cutting: Read page 5 before cutting.

- ❖ Fabric A: Theme Fabric
  Cut (6) 12-1/2" strips.
    From these strips, cut (18) 12-1/2" squares.

- ❖ Fabric B: White Fabric
  Cut (9) 2-1/2" strips.
  Cut (8) 4-1/2" strips.
    From these strips, cut (68) 4-1/2" squares.

- ❖ Fabric C: Blue Chain Fabric and Binding
  Cut (9) 2-1/2" strips.
  Cut (2) 4-1/2" strips.
    From these strips, cut (17) 4-1/2" squares.
  Cut (10) 2" strips for binding.

- ❖ Fabric D: Inner Border
  Cut (8) 2-1/2" strips.

- ❖ Fabric E: Outer Border
  Cut (8) 6" strips.

Quick and Easy Projects:

- • Matching Pillow Cases
  by Beverly Morris
  Try using your feature
  fabric and one or two
  fabric coordinates for a
  pleasing complement to
  the quilt.
- • Matching Corded Bowl
  by Patti Lee - see
  pages 134 and 135.

Quilt Size: Approx. 74" x 98"

See other fabric versions
of Marine Biology on
pages 100 and 101.

Metallic Thread Tips

*Follow these easy tips when using
Sulky Sliver and Holoshimmer™
Metallic Threads:*
- · Lower the top tension -
  sometimes to zero.
- · Place thread on vertical
  spool pin with a felt pad
  under the spool.
- · Use at least a 14/90
  metallic or topstitch
  machine needle.
- · Choose a 3.0 stitch length.
- · Use a slower sewing speed.

After a long day in the boat with Dad (Capt. Marc Noe, Joyce Drexler's son), the little fisherpeople, (Ethan and Carissa Noe) find comfort under their sparkling Marine Biology Quilt.

The Opalescent Sulky Sliver™ Metallic Thread shimmers in the Florida sunlight at the Marina in Apollo Beach, near Tampa, FL.

Book a Florida Charter

with Captain Marc Noe, contributing writer for "Florida Sport Fishing" and "Saltwater Angler" magazines, and fish the flats for Reds, Snook, Mackeral, Flounder and whatever else is running.

Or try your luck in the deeper water of Tampa Bay, fishing for Grouper, Shark, or Tarpon.

When you plan your Florida get-away, be sure to include fishing or just a day on the water watching for manatee or dolphin. It's fun for the whole family!

Visit Marc's website: www.floridafishingcharters online.com

e-mail: captmarcnoe @tampabay.rr.com

Make Block 1 *Read page 6 before beginning to sew 1/4" seams.*

1. Sew a 2-1/2" strip of white fabric and solid blue fabric together to make a strip set. Press toward the darker fabric.

Make 9

Strip Set

2. Cut into 136 strips - 2-1/2" wide.

Make 136

A

3. Sew together in sets of two, turning one side to form a checkerboard effect. Match seams. Press.

A + B = Unit 1

Unit 1
Make 68

4. Sew 2 of Unit 1 to one white 4-1/2" (C) square. Turn Unit 1 to face the other direction as illustrated. Press.

Unit 1 + C + Unit 1 = Unit 2

Make 34

5. Sew two white 4-1/2" (C) squares to one of the solid blue 4-1/2" (D) squares. Press.

C + D + C = Unit 3

Make 17

6. Sew rows together to make 17 of Block 1. Press.

Unit 2
+
Unit 3
+
Unit 2 turned
=
Block 1
Make 17

Create the Quilt Top

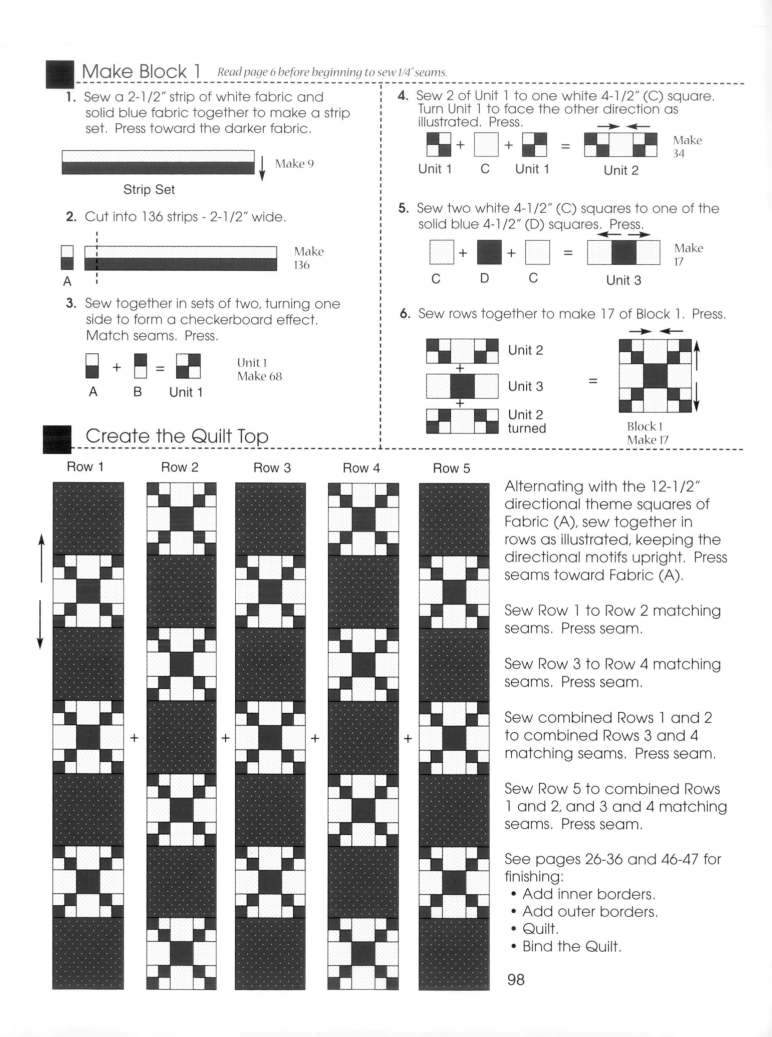

Row 1   Row 2   Row 3   Row 4   Row 5

Alternating with the 12-1/2" directional theme squares of Fabric (A), sew together in rows as illustrated, keeping the directional motifs upright. Press seams toward Fabric (A).

Sew Row 1 to Row 2 matching seams. Press seam.

Sew Row 3 to Row 4 matching seams. Press seam.

Sew combined Rows 1 and 2 to combined Rows 3 and 4 matching seams. Press seam.

Sew Row 5 to combined Rows 1 and 2, and 3 and 4 matching seams. Press seam.

See pages 26-36 and 46-47 for finishing:
- Add inner borders.
- Add outer borders.
- Quilt.
- Bind the Quilt.

98

Make Matching Pillowcases! It's Easy!

3. Sew 6 of these units together end-to-end to make a 2-1/2" x 24-1/2" Unit A. Make 2.

4. Sew 5 of these units together to make a 2-1/2" x 21-1/2" Unit B.

5. Sew a Unit A to each side of the 16-1/2" x 24-1/2" rectangle, alternating the starting and ending colors on each side.

6. Sew the Unit B to the end of this block, alternating the colors as illustrated.

7. Sew the 20-1/2" x 26-1/2" rectangle to the other side of one of the long, checked border strips, making a large pillowcase body.

8. Fold the 12-1/2" strip of accent fabric in half lengthwise and press.

9. With raw edges together, sew this piece through all layers to the end of the body unit that does not have a checkerboard strip.

10. Now is a great time to do decorative stitching. We used Sulky Sliver #8040 Opalescent to topstitch just 1/8" away from all of the seams, which gave it a soft, glistening look. Elongate the stitch length to 3mm or 4mm to get the most shimmer from the thread.

11. Fold the pillowcase, right sides together, so the cuff ends meet. Sew this envelope together along the end and then along the side.

12. Turn it right side out and admire your fine work!

Fabrics and Supplies for Pillowcase

- ✦ 1 yd. main fabric
- ✦ 1/2 yd. for cuff and accent
- ✦ Sulky Sliver™ Metallic Thread #8040 Opalescent
- ✦ Machine needle size: 14/90
- ✦ General sewing supplies - see page 3.

Cutting: Read page 5 before cutting.

- ✦ Main Fabric
    Cut (1) 2-1/2" x 42-1/2" strip.
    Cut (1) 20-1/2" x 26-1/2" rectangle.
    Cut (1) 16-1/2" x 24-1/2".

- ✦ Accent Fabric
    Cut (1) 2-1/2" x 42-1/2" strip.
    Cut (1) 12-1/2" x 42-1/2" strip.

Note: This pillowcase may be made on the serger. The seams will be sewn and finished in one pass. If the sewing machine is used, be sure to use one of the great overcast stitches that finish the seam as it is sewn. If your machine does not have a utility stitch, every seam will need to be finished with a zig-zag stitch immediately after sewing the straight stitch.

Make Checkered Border

1. Sew the 2-1/2" x 42-1/2" main fabric strip to the 2-1/2" x 42-1/2" accent strip lengthwise to create a 4-1/2" x 42-1/2" strip set.

2. Cut this strip set into (17) 2-1/2" x 4-1/2" units.

French Borders

Another version of Marine Biology
See closeup of quilting on page 18.

Credits: Level: Beginner   Quilt designed and pieced by: Beverly Morris   Quilted by: Evelyn Byler using Sulky 30 wt. Multi-Color Rayon Thread #2207.   Finished size: 78" x 102" Featured Fabric: Thimbleberries by RJR. Use same instructions and measurements starting on Page 96.

It's so much fun to make a coordinating Fabric Rag Bowl to match your quilt. Use some of all the left-over fabrics to make it unique. Stitching it together with Sulky 12 wt. Blendables adds even more texture.

Using a line of fabrics from one designer gives you a perfect palette from which to choose. And quilting it with Sulky Multi-color 30 wt. (heavier) Rayon makes it perfect! There are also many new Sulky Cotton Blendables that complement Thimbleberries fabrics.

Woodland Flannel Another fabric version of the Marine Biology Quilt.

Credits: Level: Beginner Original Pattern by: Beverly Morris Pieced by: Nancy Bryant
Quilted by: Evelyn Byler using Sulky 30 wt. Rayon #567 Butterfly Gold, #1001 White, and
#1058 Tawny Brown. Sulky Holoshimmer Copper in ditches. Featured Fabric: Alexander Henry
Use same instructions and measurements starting on page 96. Finished Size: 74" x 98"

Perfect for that cabin in the woods or that man in your life!
Make the borders of your quilt the size that best suits your needs.

Sophisticated Squares

Block 1
Make 13

Block 2
Make 12 ▶

Fabrics & Supplies Needed for Quilt

All strips are cut across the fabric, selvage to selvage, assuming 42" of usable fabric. Cut off all selvages.

❖ 2-1/4 yds. fabric A; 2 yds. fabric B; 1-3/4 yds. fabric C; 1 yd. fabric D
❖ 1-1/2 yards of a large print E with a background the same color as fabric A to create a floating effect in block 2
❖ 1-3/4 yds. for border - Fabric A
❖ 1 yd. for bias binding - Fabric A
❖ 8 yds. (42") or 2-7/8 yds. (108") for backing
❖ Hobbs 20/80 Batting, at least 100" x 100"
❖ Sulky 12 wt. & 30 wt. Cotton Blendables Thread
❖ Machine needle size: 14/90 or 16/100
❖ General sewing supplies - see page 3

Credits:

Level: Intermediate
Quilt designed by:
Beverly Morris
Pieced by: Joyce Drexler
Quilted by: Evelyn Byler
Featured Fabric: Hoffman Batiks

See the same quilt using alternative fabric choices on page 107.

Quilt Size:
Approx. 88" sq.

Smaller version on page 108.

Cutting: Read page 5 before cutting. Make a Fabric Key - page 8.

❖ **Fabric A: Dark/Dark**
(same color as the featured print's background)
 Cut (6) 5-1/4" strips. From these, cut (48) 5-1/4" squares.
 Cut (7) 3-1/2" strips. From these, cut (52) 3-1/2" x 5" strips.
 Cut (9) 2" strips.
 Cut (10) 5" strips for border.

❖ **Fabric B: Dark**
 Cut (21) 2" strips.
 Cut (6) 4-3/4" strips. From these, cut (48) 4-3/4" squares.

❖ **Fabric C: Medium**
 Cut (28) 2" strips.

❖ **Fabric D: Light**
 Cut (17) 2" strips.

❖ **Fabric E: Large Feature Print**
 Cut (4) 12" strips. From these, cut (12) 12" squares.

Wouldn't this quilt be perfect for that man in your life?

1. Sew 2 strip sets as illustrated. Press seams toward the darker fabric. Cut into (26) 2" pieced strips "A".

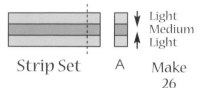

Strip Set   A   Make 26

Light
Medium
Light

2. Sew a strip set as illustrated. Press seams toward the darker fabric. Cut into (13) 2" pieced strips "B".

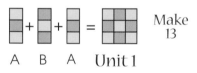

Strip Set   B   Make 13

Medium
Light
Medium

3. Sew a 2" pieced strip "A" to both sides of a strip "B" as illustrated to make a 9-patch Unit 1. Make 13. Press toward dark.

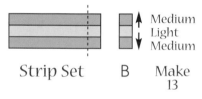

A   B   A   Unit 1   Make 13

4. Sew 6 strip sets as illustrated below. Press toward the darkest fabric. Cut into (104) 2" pieced strips "C".

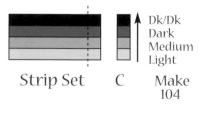

Strip Set   C   Make 104

Dk/Dk
Dark
Medium
Light

5. Sew 6 strip sets as illustrated below. Press toward the lightest fabric. Cut into (104) 2" pieced strips "D".

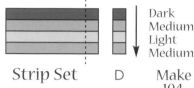

Strip Set   D   Make 104

Dark
Medium
Light
Medium

6. Sew 2 each of the pieced strips "C" and "D" together as illustrated below into a 16-patch Unit 2. Make 52. Press seams all in the same direction.

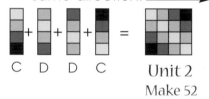

C   D   D   C   Unit 2
Make 52

7. Sew 3 strip sets as illustrated. Press seams toward the center strip. Cut into (52) 2" pieced strips "E".

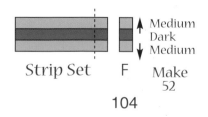

Strip Set   E   Make 52

Dark
Dark/Dark
Dark

8. Sew 3 strip sets as illustrated. Press seams toward the outside strips. Cut into (52) 2" pieced strips "F".

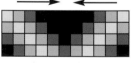

Strip Set   F   Make 52

Medium
Dark
Medium

9. Sew a pieced strip set "E" and "F" together as illustrated below to make Unit 3. Make 52. Press seams as indicated.

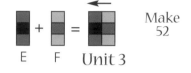

E   F   Unit 3   Make 52

10. Sew a Unit 3 to the side of the fabric "A" 3-1/2" x 5" rectangle as illustrated below to make Unit 4. Make 52. Press seams toward the rectangle.

Unit 3   Unit 4   Make 52

11. Sew a Unit 2 to a Unit 4. Sew combination to another turned Unit 2 as illustrated below to make Unit 5. Make 26. Press toward the center.

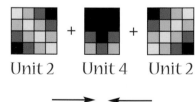

Unit 2   Unit 4   Unit 2

Unit 5
Make 26

12. Sew a Unit 4 to a Unit 1. Sew that combination to another turned Unit 4 to make Unit 6. Make 13. Press to the outside.

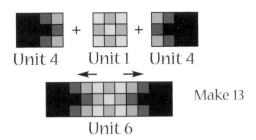

Unit 4   +   Unit 1   +   Unit 4

Make 13

Unit 6

13. Sew a Unit 5 to a Unit 6. Sew them to another turned Unit 5 as illustrated below to make **Block 1.** Press. Block should measure 17" square.

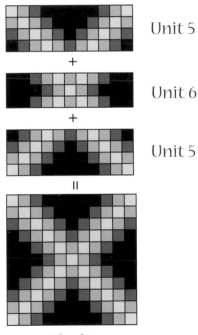

Unit 5

+

Unit 6

+

Unit 5

||

Block 1
Make 13

1. Locate the (48) 5-1/4" squares of Dk/Dk Fabric A. Cut each one diagonally to make 2 triangles.

Make 96 Triangles

2. Attach 2 of these triangles to each of the (48) 4-3/4" squares of fabric B as illustrated below to make 48 Triangle Unit 1. Press toward the triangles.

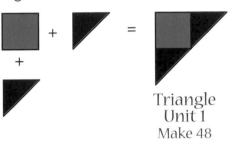

+   =

+

Triangle Unit 1
Make 48

3. Sew one Triangle Unit 1 to each of the 4 sides of a 12" large print square to make a 17" Block 2. Make 12. Press toward the large square.

Block 2
Make 12

■ Make 10 Sets of Block 1 sewn to Block 2

> *Tip:* After ironing and blocking Block 1, if it came out slightly smaller than Block 2, trim Block 2 to the same size as Block 1.

1. Place a Block 1 and a Block 2, right sides together. Pin together <u>matching edges</u>. **Note that the seams from the patchwork in Block 1 and Block 2 are <u>not</u> designed to match exactly.** Sew 10 Sets and press seam.

 +

Make 10 Sets of Block 1 and Block 2 sewn together.

■ Create the Quilt Top

1. Refer to the finished quilt top illustration below.
   Row 1 - Sew 2 block set 1's (above) together and add one block 1.
   Row 2 - Sew one block 2 to 2 block set 1's sewn together.
   Row 3 - Repeat row 1.
   Row 4 - Repeat row 2.
   Row 5 - Repeat row 1.

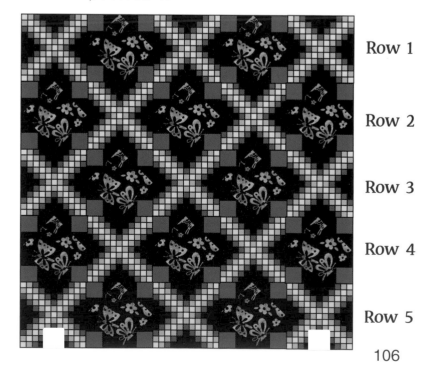

Row 1

Row 2

Row 3

Row 4

Row 5

■ Add Borders
Refer to page 26

■ Layer
Refer to page 28

■ Quilt
Refer to page 30

■ Bind
Refer to page 46

Sophisticated Batik   Another version of Sophisticated Squares

Credits: Level: Intermediate   Quilt designed by: Beverly Morris   Pieced by: Joyce Drexler
Quilted by: Evelyn Byler using Sulky 30 wt. Cotton Blendables #4020 and #4010, and Sulky Sliver™
#8010 Lt. Copper for stitching-in-the-ditch.   Featured Fabrics: Hoffman Batiks   Finished size:
88"square. Use the same instructions and measurements starting on page 102.

Small Sophisticated Squares

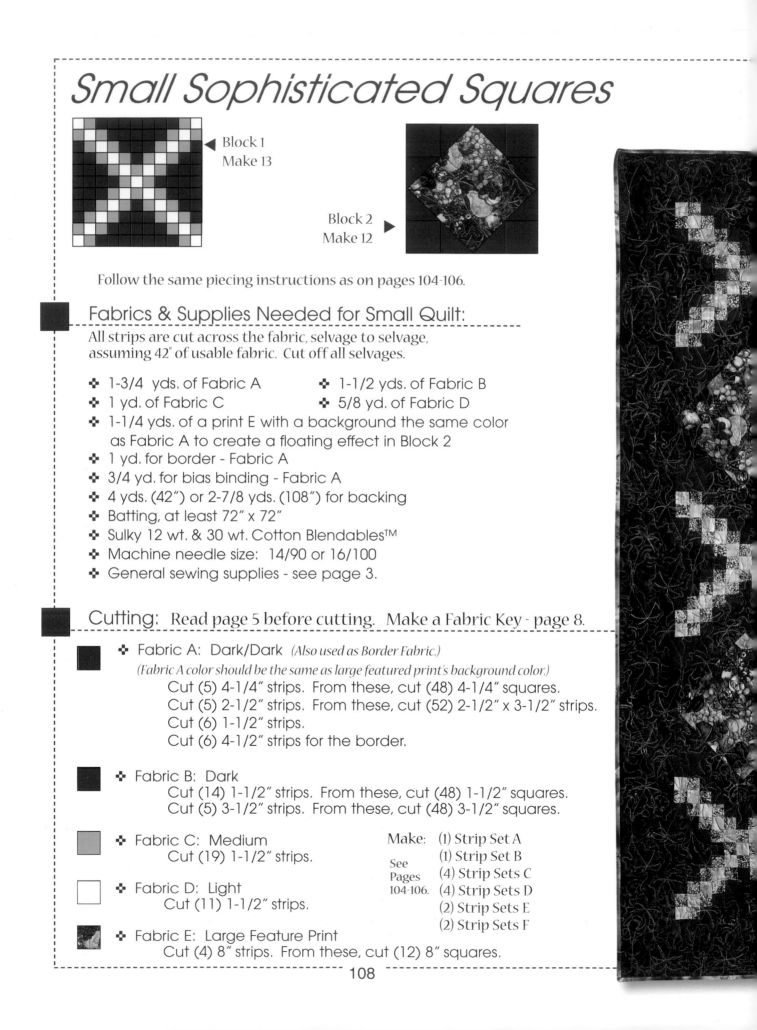

◄ Block 1
Make 13

Block 2 ►
Make 12

Follow the same piecing instructions as on pages 104-106.

Fabrics & Supplies Needed for Small Quilt:

All strips are cut across the fabric, selvage to selvage,
assuming 42" of usable fabric. Cut off all selvages.

- 1-3/4 yds. of Fabric A
- 1-1/2 yds. of Fabric B
- 1 yd. of Fabric C
- 5/8 yd. of Fabric D
- 1-1/4 yds. of a print E with a background the same color
  as Fabric A to create a floating effect in Block 2
- 1 yd. for border - Fabric A
- 3/4 yd. for bias binding - Fabric A
- 4 yds. (42") or 2-7/8 yds. (108") for backing
- Batting, at least 72" x 72"
- Sulky 12 wt. & 30 wt. Cotton Blendables™
- Machine needle size: 14/90 or 16/100
- General sewing supplies - see page 3.

Cutting: Read page 5 before cutting. Make a Fabric Key - page 8.

- Fabric A: Dark/Dark *(Also used as Border Fabric.)*
  (Fabric A color should be the same as large featured print's background color.)
  Cut (5) 4-1/4" strips. From these, cut (48) 4-1/4" squares.
  Cut (5) 2-1/2" strips. From these, cut (52) 2-1/2" x 3-1/2" strips.
  Cut (6) 1-1/2" strips.
  Cut (6) 4-1/2" strips for the border.

- Fabric B: Dark
  Cut (14) 1-1/2" strips. From these, cut (48) 1-1/2" squares.
  Cut (5) 3-1/2" strips. From these, cut (48) 3-1/2" squares.

- Fabric C: Medium
  Cut (19) 1-1/2" strips.

- Fabric D: Light
  Cut (11) 1-1/2" strips.

Make: (1) Strip Set A
(1) Strip Set B
See (4) Strip Sets C
Pages (4) Strip Sets D
104-106. (2) Strip Sets E
(2) Strip Sets F

- Fabric E: Large Feature Print
  Cut (4) 8" strips. From these, cut (12) 8" squares.

Credits:
Level: Intermediate   Quilt designed by: Beverly Morris
Quilted by: Evelyn Byler using Sulky Cotton Blendables #4009
Foliage   Featured Fabric: Hoffman Batiks

Quilt Size:
Approx. 63" sq.

Audition different spools of Blendables to see what might make your quilt pop with excitement and depth!
 It's fun

Try drizzling the thread from the spool to see what looks best.

Tickled Pink

Credits: Level: Intermediate   Quilt designed by: Bevelry Morris   Pieced by: Nancy Bryant using the Small Sophisticated Squares measurements   Quilted by: Evelyn Byler using Sulky Holoshimmer #6003 Lt. Gold

Projects: • Pieced Rug - page 115
• Christmas Tree Skirt - page 116
• Mantle or Shelf Cover - page 112
• Corded Baskets - page 142

*Wouldn't it
be nice if . . .
you could take a
nice long, restful,
scented bubble bath
surrounded by
beautifully
quilted items?*

*And . . .
you could drink
a little wine,
enjoy a little
candlelight,
and dream about
what you wanted
Santa to bring
you for Christmas?*

*And you made it
all come true!*

Angel Mantle Cover

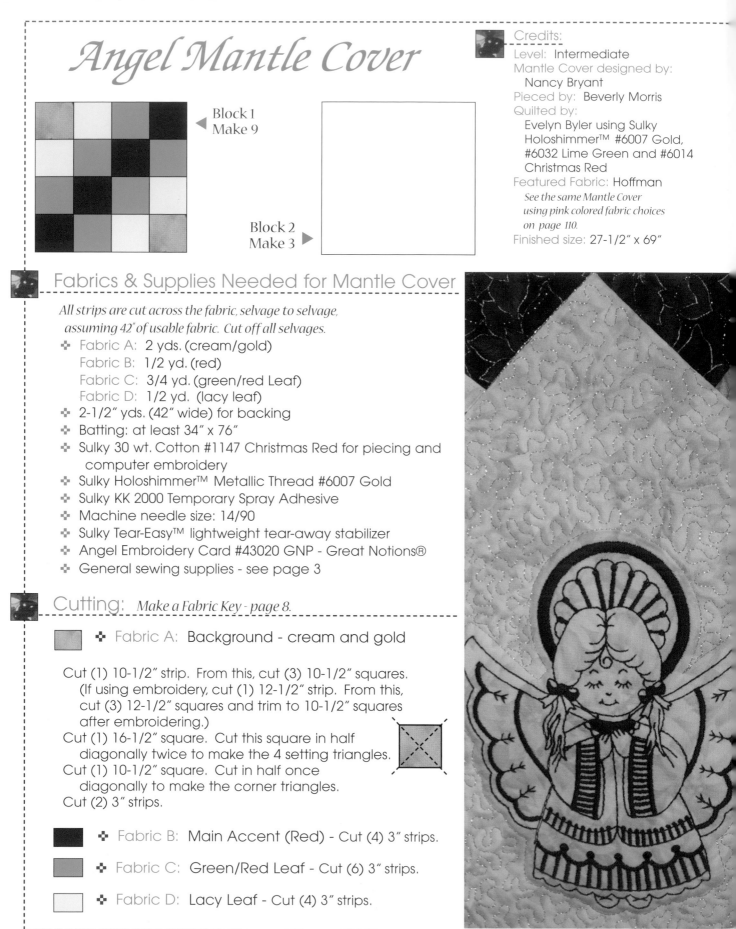

Block 1
Make 9

Block 2
Make 3

Credits:
Level: Intermediate
Mantle Cover designed by:
  Nancy Bryant
Pieced by: Beverly Morris
Quilted by:
  Evelyn Byler using Sulky
  Holoshimmer™ #6007 Gold,
  #6032 Lime Green and #6014
  Christmas Red
Featured Fabric: Hoffman
  *See the same Mantle Cover
  using pink colored fabric choices
  on page 110.*
Finished size: 27-1/2" x 69"

Fabrics & Supplies Needed for Mantle Cover

*All strips are cut across the fabric, selvage to selvage,
assuming 42" of usable fabric. Cut off all selvages.*

- Fabric A: 2 yds. (cream/gold)
  Fabric B: 1/2 yd. (red)
  Fabric C: 3/4 yd. (green/red Leaf)
  Fabric D: 1/2 yd. (lacy leaf)
- 2-1/2" yds. (42" wide) for backing
- Batting: at least 34" x 76"
- Sulky 30 wt. Cotton #1147 Christmas Red for piecing and
  computer embroidery
- Sulky Holoshimmer™ Metallic Thread #6007 Gold
- Sulky KK 2000 Temporary Spray Adhesive
- Machine needle size: 14/90
- Sulky Tear-Easy™ lightweight tear-away stabilizer
- Angel Embroidery Card #43020 GNP - Great Notions®
- General sewing supplies - see page 3

Cutting: *Make a Fabric Key - page 8.*

- Fabric A: Background - cream and gold

Cut (1) 10-1/2" strip. From this, cut (3) 10-1/2" squares.
(If using embroidery, cut (1) 12-1/2" strip. From this,
cut (3) 12-1/2" squares and trim to 10-1/2" squares
after embroidering.)
Cut (1) 16-1/2" square. Cut this square in half
diagonally twice to make the 4 setting triangles.
Cut (1) 10-1/2" square. Cut in half once
diagonally to make the corner triangles.
Cut (2) 3" strips.

- Fabric B: Main Accent (Red) - Cut (4) 3" strips.

- Fabric C: Green/Red Leaf - Cut (6) 3" strips.

- Fabric D: Lacy Leaf - Cut (4) 3" strips.

Computer Embroidery

• *See page 118 for instructions.*

Construct Block 1

1. Sew the 3" strips into the following strip set "A". Make 2.

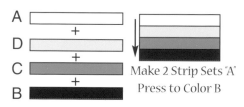

Make 2 Strip Sets "A"
Press to Color B

2. Cut the two strip sets "A" into (18) 3" x 10-1/2" Unit 1.

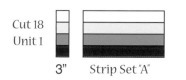

Cut 18
Unit 1

3"   Strip Set "A"

3. Sew the 3" strips into the following strip set "B". Make 2.

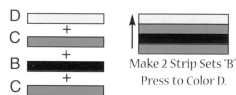

Make 2 Strip Sets "B"
Press to Color D.

4. Cut the two strip sets "B" into (18) 3" x 10-1/2" Unit 2.

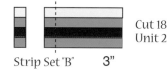

Cut 18
Unit 2

Strip Set "B"   3"

5. Assemble the Units into a 10-1/2" square Block 1. Make 9.

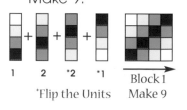

1   2   *2   *1   Block 1
*Flip the Units   Make 9

Assemble the Mantle Cover

1. Assemble the patchwork blocks into five rows with the triangles as illustrated. Sew the Rows together, nesting the seam allowances. Note - triangles will be larger than needed. Trim to size after stitching.

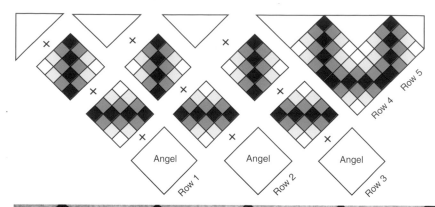

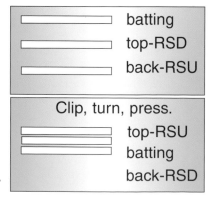

Flip & Sew Method of Layering & Finishing

1. Spray KK 2000 on the wrong side of the mantel top and smooth batting over it. Trim batting to match top. Spray KK 2000 on the right side of the backing fabric. Place the top, right sides together, with the backing fabric. Trim backing to match top. Using a 1/4" seam allowance, stitch around the entire mantle cover, leaving a 13" opening on the long, straight side to turn.

2. Clip into points, turn and press. Hand stitch opening closed. Using Sulky Holoshimmer #6007 Gold and a quarter-inch foot, stitch around the entire piece 1/4" from the edge.

batting
top-RSD
back-RSU

Clip, turn, press.
top-RSU
batting
back-RSD

Quilt it!   See page 30.

Strip and Flip Accent Rug

Credits:
Level: Beginner - Easy
Accent Rug designed by:
  Beverly Morris
Featured Fabric: Hoffman
Finished Size: 20-1/2" x 42"
See additional photo on page 110.

Fabrics & Supplies Needed for Rug:

All strips are cut across the fabric, selvage to selvage, assuming 42" of usable fabric. Cut off all selvages.

- 1/2 yd. each of 7 coordinating fabrics
- 1/2 yd. for binding
- Batting - at least 21" x 54"
- Sulky KK 2000 Temporary Spray Adhesive
- Machine Needle Size: 14/90 Topstitch
- Rug grip material for use under the rug to prevent slipping
- General sewing supplies - see page 3

Cutting: Make a Fabric Key - page 8.

- Cut (6) 2-1/2" strips from each of the 7 fabrics. Cut these strips in half so each measures 2-1/2" x 21" long.

- Cut (21) 2-1/2" x 21" strips of batting.

Sewing:

1. Make a beginning sandwich by layering (spray KK 2000 between layers) one of your fabrics as follows:
   C. Fabric (right side down)
   B. Batting
   A. Fabric (right side up)

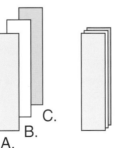

2. With right sides together, layer (spray KK 2000 between layers):
   - The next strip - face up
   - The beginning sandwich
   - Another strip - face down
   - A strip of batting - on top

3. Using a 1/4" seam, sew down the length; smooth strips open as illustrated.

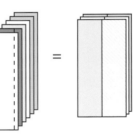

4. Continue adding strips until the rug is the length desired.

5. Add the binding as described on page 46.

6. Place a rug grip material under the rug to prevent slipping when in use.

Angel Tree Skirt or Table Cover

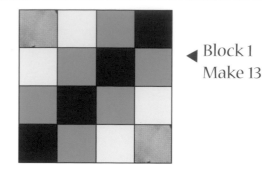

◀ Block 1
Make 13

Fabrics & Supplies for Tree Skirt or Table Cover

All strips are cut across the fabric, selvage to selvage, assuming 42" of usable fabric. Cut off all selvages.

- ✤ Fabric A: 2 yds. (cream/gold)
- ✤ Fabric B: 1/2 yd. (red)
- ✤ Fabric C: 3/4 yd. (green/red leaf)
- ✤ Fabric D: 1/2 yd. (lacy leaf)
- ✤ 4 yds. (42" wide) for backing
- ✤ Batting at least 67" x 67"
- ✤ Sulky 30 wt. Cotton Thread #1147 Christmas Red for piecing and computer embroidery
- ✤ Sulky Holoshimmer™ #6007 Gold
- ✤ Machine Needle Size: 14/90 Topstitch
- ✤ Sulky Tear Easy™ lightweight tear-away stabilizer
- ✤ Redwork Angel Embroidery Card #43020 GNP by Great Notions
- ✤ General sewing supplies - see page 3

Credits:

Level: Intermediate
Tree Skirt designed by:
  Nancy Bryant
Quilted by:
  Evelyn Byler using Sulky
  Holoshimmer™ #6007
  Gold and #6032 Lime
Featured Fabric:
  Hoffman
  *See the same Tree
  Skirt using pink
  fabrics on page 110.*

Tree Skirt Size:

Approx. 60" x 60"
  point-to-point

Cutting: Read page 5. Set up a Fabric Key - page 8.

- ✤ **Fabric A: Background - cream/gold**
  Cut (2) 10-1/2" strips. From these, cut (8) 10-1/2" squares. (Or, if embroidering Angels, cut (2) 12-1/2" strips; then cut (4) 12-1/2" squares and, after embroidering on as many as you wish, trim to 10-1/2" squares.)
  Cut (1) 16-1/2" strip. From this, cut (2) 16-1/2" squares. (If embroidering angels, cut (2) 17-1/2" squares; then cut them in half diagonally; embroider an angel on 3 of these triangles. See page 118.)   Set extra triangle aside for now.
  Cut (2) 3" strips.

- ✤ **Fabric B: Main accent red**
  Cut (4) 3" strips.

- ✤ **Fabric C: Green/red leaf**
  Cut (6) 3" strips.

- ✤ **Fabric D: Lacy leaf** - Cut (4) 3" strips.

Computer Embroidery

· Use Joyce Drexler's 5" x 7" *Redwork Angel Embroidery Card #43020 GNP by Great Notions.*

· Put Sulky 30 wt. Cotton #1147 *Christmas Red on both the top and in the bobbin. Because cotton thread does fuzz, clean the machine often.*

· Use a size 14/90 topstitch *needle.*

· Center the *12-1/2" squares of background fabric used for the embroideries on point as illustrated; after embroidering, trim them to 10-1/2" squares.*

· Use the triangles cut from the *17-1/2" squares for the (3) triangle embroideries and trim them to 16-1/2" after embroidering.*

· Center the embroideries on *the triangles 4-1/2" from the long side edge.*

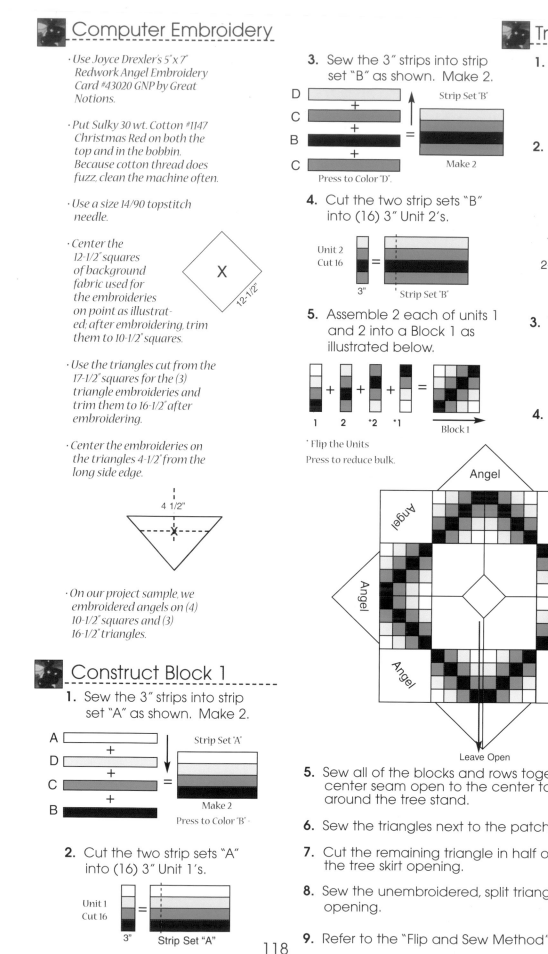

· On our project sample, we *embroidered angels on (4) 10-1/2" squares and (3) 16-1/2" triangles.*

Construct Block 1

1. Sew the 3" strips into strip set "A" as shown. Make 2.

Strip Set "A"
Make 2
Press to Color "B"

2. Cut the two strip sets "A" into (16) 3" Unit 1's.

Unit 1
Cut 16
3"   Strip Set "A"

3. Sew the 3" strips into strip set "B" as shown. Make 2.

Strip Set "B"
Make 2
Press to Color "D".

4. Cut the two strip sets "B" into (16) 3" Unit 2's.

Unit 2
Cut 16
3"   Strip Set "B"

5. Assemble 2 each of units 1 and 2 into a Block 1 as illustrated below.

1   2   *2   *1   Block 1

* Flip the Units
Press to reduce bulk.

Tree Skirt Assembly

1. Along the top of (4) of the 10-1/2" Fabric A squares, mark a dot 2-1/2" from the corner.

2. Mark a second dot 2-1/2" down the side from the same corner of the square.

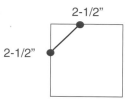

2-1/2"
2-1/2"

3. To allow for the center of the tree skirt, trim away the corner on all 4 squares from dot to dot.

4. Assemble just the patchwork blocks with the background squares into four rows as illustrated.

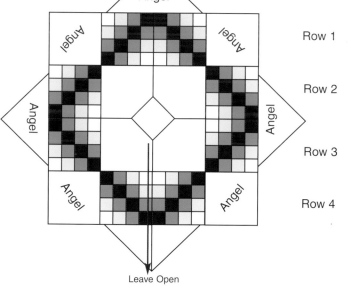

Row 1

Row 2

Row 3

Row 4

Leave Open

5. Sew all of the blocks and rows together leaving one center seam open to the center to allow it to be placed around the tree stand.

6. Sew the triangles next to the patchwork blocks.

7. Cut the remaining triangle in half once more to continue the tree skirt opening.

8. Sew the unembroidered, split triangles next to the seam opening.

9. Refer to the "Flip and Sew Method" for layering. Page 114.

Angels in my Cabin

Block 1
Make 6 ▶

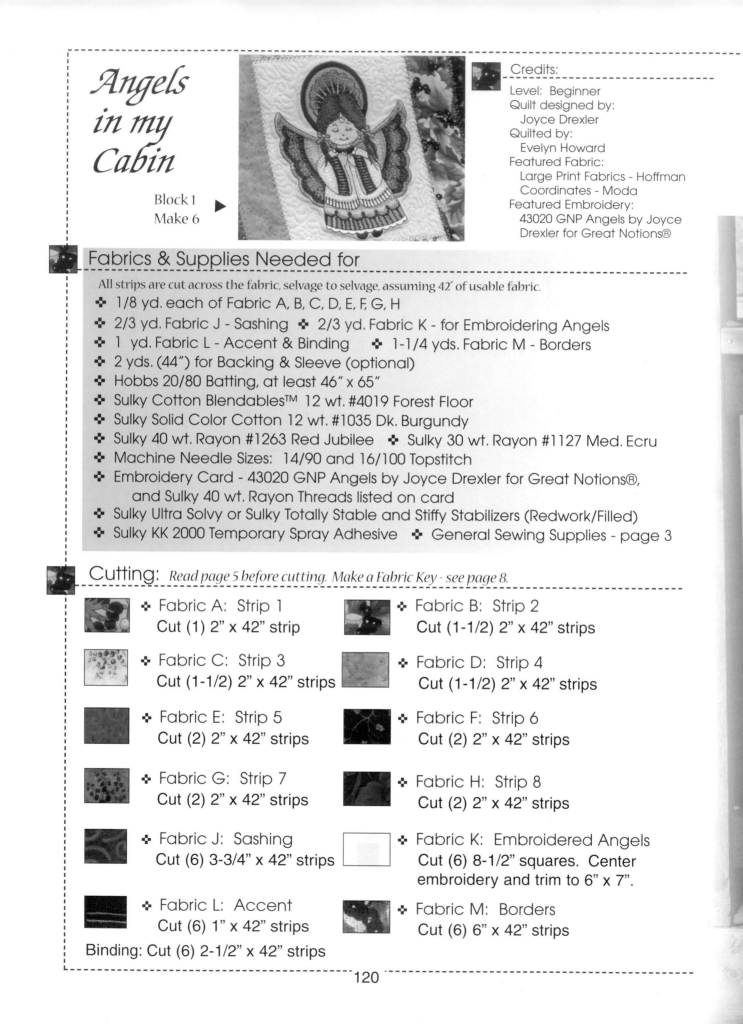

Credits:
Level: Beginner
Quilt designed by:
  Joyce Drexler
Quilted by:
  Evelyn Howard
Featured Fabric:
  Large Print Fabrics - Hoffman
  Coordinates - Moda
Featured Embroidery:
  43020 GNP Angels by Joyce
  Drexler for Great Notions®

Fabrics & Supplies Needed for

All strips are cut across the fabric, selvage to selvage, assuming 42" of usable fabric.

- ❖ 1/8 yd. each of Fabric A, B, C, D, E, F, G, H
- ❖ 2/3 yd. Fabric J - Sashing ❖ 2/3 yd. Fabric K - for Embroidering Angels
- ❖ 1 yd. Fabric L - Accent & Binding ❖ 1-1/4 yds. Fabric M - Borders
- ❖ 2 yds. (44") for Backing & Sleeve (optional)
- ❖ Hobbs 20/80 Batting, at least 46" x 65"
- ❖ Sulky Cotton Blendables™ 12 wt. #4019 Forest Floor
- ❖ Sulky Solid Color Cotton 12 wt. #1035 Dk. Burgundy
- ❖ Sulky 40 wt. Rayon #1263 Red Jubilee ❖ Sulky 30 wt. Rayon #1127 Med. Ecru
- ❖ Machine Needle Sizes: 14/90 and 16/100 Topstitch
- ❖ Embroidery Card - 43020 GNP Angels by Joyce Drexler for Great Notions®,
     and Sulky 40 wt. Rayon Threads listed on card
- ❖ Sulky Ultra Solvy or Sulky Totally Stable and Stiffy Stabilizers (Redwork/Filled)
- ❖ Sulky KK 2000 Temporary Spray Adhesive ❖ General Sewing Supplies - page 3

Cutting: *Read page 5 before cutting. Make a Fabric Key - see page 8.*

- ❖ Fabric A: Strip 1
  Cut (1) 2" x 42" strip

- ❖ Fabric B: Strip 2
  Cut (1-1/2) 2" x 42" strips

- ❖ Fabric C: Strip 3
  Cut (1-1/2) 2" x 42" strips

- ❖ Fabric D: Strip 4
  Cut (1-1/2) 2" x 42" strips

- ❖ Fabric E: Strip 5
  Cut (2) 2" x 42" strips

- ❖ Fabric F: Strip 6
  Cut (2) 2" x 42" strips

- ❖ Fabric G: Strip 7
  Cut (2) 2" x 42" strips

- ❖ Fabric H: Strip 8
  Cut (2) 2" x 42" strips

- ❖ Fabric J: Sashing
  Cut (6) 3-3/4" x 42" strips

- ❖ Fabric K: Embroidered Angels
  Cut (6) 8-1/2" squares. Center
  embroidery and trim to 6" x 7".

- ❖ Fabric L: Accent
  Cut (6) 1" x 42" strips

- ❖ Fabric M: Borders
  Cut (6) 6" x 42" strips

Binding: Cut (6) 2-1/2" x 42" strips

Other Projects - Kitchen Goodies --- Find patterns on www.sulky.com website

- Toaster Cover - page 125
- Blender Cover - page 125
- Dish Towels - page 127
- Potted Plant Wrap - page 131
- Corded Scubber Holder - page 135
- Hot Pads - page 133
- Soap or Lotion Covers - page 129

Finished Wallhanging or Throw Size: Approx. 43" x 61"

Embroider the Angels

1. Set up the sewing machine with the Embroidery Unit. Use Embroidery Card - 43020 GNP Angels. Assemble Sulky 40 wt. Rayon Threads listed.
2. For <u>Filled Angels</u>: Iron a similar size piece of Sulky Totally Stable Stabilizer onto the back of each of the (6) 8-1/2" squares of Fabric K. Lightly spray Sulky KK 2000 Temporary Spray Adhesive onto two layers of Sulky Stiffy Stabilizer and adhere them onto the back of the Totally Stable. Repeat for each square.
   For <u>Redwork Angels:</u> Cut a similar size piece of Sulky Ultra Solvy as the fabric. Lightly moisten the Ultra Solvy with a damp sponge and gently smooth the fabric onto the moistened Ultra Solvy. Allow it to dry.
3. Hoop and embroider each Angel. Remove the stabilizer: for Redwork Angel, by rinsing, drying and pressing. For the Filled Angel, tear away one layer at a time.

Strip-piece the Angel Blocks

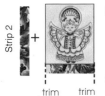

1. Center the angel embroidery and trim each angel block to 6" x 7".
2. Lay strip 1 right side down at the bottom of the first angel block. Match the edges and stitch them together with a 1/4" seam. Repeat sewing the other 5 angel blocks onto this strip, using the chain piecing method (see page 6).
3. Press seam allowances toward strip 1.
4. Trim off strip 1 flush with each angel block as illustrated below.

5. Place strip 2 on the side of an angel block as illustrated and repeat 2-4 to stitch all 6 angels onto this strip.
6. Continue adding strips 3-8, repeating steps 2 through 4 as illustrated.

Add the Sashing Strips

1. Cut 4 sashing strips 3-3/4" x 12" from fabric J.
2. Sew sashing strips between 3 different pieced angel blocks. Trim strips flush to the pieced blocks.
3. Repeat for 3 other pieced angel blocks.
4. Cut enough 3-3/4" sashing strips from fabric J to first sew one sashing strip between these 2 units, followed by one on each side, then one on the top and bottom, as illustrated below.

122

Add the Folded Accent Strips

1. Piece the striped accent strips "L" together to make the lengths needed.
2. Fold the accent strip lengthwise with the wrong sides together and pin it to the bottom and top sashings so all edges are flush together. Sew together using an edge foot and *scant* 1/4" seam.
3. Repeat, applying the accent strips to the left and right sashings.

Add the Mitered Borders

1. Using the 6" border strips - fabric "M", follow "Mitered Border" instructions on page 27 to add these borders. Press seams toward borders.

Layer Quilt - see page 28

Machine Quilting - Redwork Version

1. Baste the quilt sandwich.
2. Stitch in the ditches of the outer seams of the block using Sulky 12 wt. Solid Color Cotton #1035 Dk. Burgundy on top and the matching 30 wt. Cotton in the bobbin. Use the same thread and a wide feather stitch (5.0W; 2.5L) to stitch over the seam lines of the inner strips around the angel blocks.
3. Using Sulky 40 wt. or 30 wt. Rayon #1127 Med. Ecru, echo quilt the width of the foot around each angel. Then, free-motion stipple quilt from the edge of the echo quilting (see photo above right) to the log cabin strips.
4. Use Sulky 12 wt. Cotton Blendables #4019 Forest Floor to "Meander Quilt" (see page 34) the sashing strips.
5. Using Sulky 12 wt. Solid Color Cotton #1035 Dk. Burgundy, quilt the borders with a Meandering Stitch.

Machine Quilting - Filled Version

1. Baste the quilt sandwich.
2. Quilt as in #2 above except use Sulky Holoshimmer #6007 Gold on the top and Sulky Polyester Clear Invisible in the bobbin. See p. 24.
3. Same as above.
4. Quilt as in #4 above except use Sulky Sliver #8040 Opalescent on the top.
5. Use Sulky Holoshimmer #6007 Gold to "Outline Quilt" following the printed holly leaves.

Add Striped Binding - see page 46

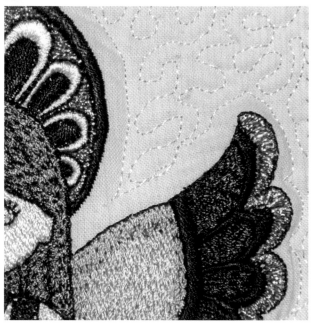

Closeup of "Echo" and "Stipple Quilting" around angel with Sulky 40 wt. Rayon Thread.

Closeup of "Meandering", "Stitching in the Ditch", and "Outline Quilting" in the border of the Filled Angel Quilt using Sulky Holoshimmer Metallic Thread.

Angels in the Kitchen

124

Kitchen Goodies

Fun with Diamond and Channel Quilting!

Credits:
Level: Beginner
Designed & Quilted by: Pam Laba
Featured Fabric: Hoffman Christmas
    Print and Moda Fabrics
Featured Embroidery: 43020 GNP
    Angels Collection 1 by Joyce Drexler
    for Great Notions®

Fabrics & Supplies Needed for Quilted Blender & Toaster Covers

All strips are cut across the fabric, selvage to selvage, assuming 42" of usable fabric.

- ❖ Simplicity Pattern 8693 or Blender & 4-slot Toaster Cover pattern of your choice
- ❖ 12" x 18" Fabric for front and back pattern pieces - Blender Cover
- ❖ 12" x 18" Fabric for front and back pattern pieces - Toaster Cover (This will fit a large, wide, 4-slice toaster.)
- ❖ 11" x 42" Fabric for gusset - Blender Cover
- ❖ 11" x 42" Fabric for gusset - Toaster Cover

Note: All pattern pieces can be found at www.sulky.com

- ❖ Muslin linings - cut front & back pieces 12" x 18" & gusset 11" x 42" - Blender Cover
- ❖ Muslin linings - cut front & back pieces 12" x 18" & gusset 11" x 42" - Toaster Cover
- ❖ 10" x 15" neutral fabric for each angel embroidery; trim to 6" x 7" after embroidery
- ❖ Sulky KK 2000 Temporary Spray Adhesive   ❖ Sulky Bobbin Thread
- ❖ Warm and Natural Cotton Batting cut same sizes as muslin lining
- ❖ 3-1/2 yds. of finished double-folded bias binding from a contrasting fabric for each
- ❖ 2" x 10" strips of 4 contrasting fabrics for strips around angel embroideries
- ❖ Sulky Holoshimmer #6007 Gold   ❖ Sulky 40 wt. Rayon Thread for embroideries
- ❖ Sulky 40 wt. Rayon #1263 Red Jubilee - to match binding
- ❖ Machine needle size: 14/90   ❖ Machine quilt guide   ❖ Chalk marker
- ❖ Embroidery card - 43020 GNP Angels by Joyce Drexler for Great Notions®
- ❖ Sulky Ultra Solvy™ Stabilizer for embroidering Redwork Angels
- ❖ Sulky Totally Stable™ and Stiffy™ Stabilizers for embroidering filled Angels

Embroider Angel - See page 122 for instructions.

Preparation of Quilted Front, Back and Gusset Pieces

1. For the front, back and gusset of cover: lightly spray Sulky KK 2000 onto the batting and smooth it onto the muslin lining fabric. Then, spray the top side of the batting and smooth the fabric onto it.
2. To create lines for the diamond quilting pattern on the front and back, mark diagonal lines with chalk 1-1/2" apart in both directions, or just mark one line each way and use a quilting guide.
3. To create lines for channel quilting, mark diagonal lines on the gusset 1-1/2" apart in one direction or the other, or use a quilting guide.
4. Thread the top with Sulky Holoshimmer #6007 Gold and put Sulky Bobbin Thread in the bobbin. See tips for using Metallic Threads on page 24.
5. Quilt on the drawn lines using a 3 mm long straight stitch.
6. Use pattern pieces to cut out front, back and gusset.

Front
&
Back

Gusset ➤

Strip Piece Log Cabin Angel Applique (1/4" seam allowance).

1. Center and trim embroidered angel fabric to measure 6" x 7".
2. Fold and press the (4) 2" x 10" log cabin strips in half lengthwise, wrong sides together, to form a trim.
3. Using regular sewing thread or Sulky 30 wt. Cotton, sew the first of the strips to the bottom edge of a 6" side of the angel embroidery.
4. Trim both ends to be even with the 6" angel fabric and press the seam toward the strip.
5. Add the second strip to the left of the angel and the first strip.
6. Trim both ends to be even with the 7" side and press seam toward the second strip.
7. Continue adding the third and fourth strips, trimming and pressing as above.

Apply the Angel Applique

1. Find the front center of the right side of the blender cover (or toaster cover) and the log cabin, embroidered angel fabric.
2. Spray KK 2000 onto the wrong side of the log cabin, angel applique and smooth in place, matching centers.
3. Thread the top with Sulky Holoshimmer #6007 Gold and put Sulky Bobbin Thread in the bobbin. See tips for using Metallic Threads on page 24. Using a feather stitch (2.5 mm long and 5 mm wide), stitch on the seam lines of the log cabin.
4. Feather stitch on the folds of the log cabin strips, appliquéing them to the cover fronts.

Make Bias Binding

1. Cut fabric on the bias into 2" strips for binding.
2. Stitch cut strips together lengthwise using Sulky 30 wt. Cotton Thread.
3. Press bias binding in half lengthwise (wrong sides together) to create double-folded binding.

Construct the Covers

1. Apply binding to the lower edges of the front, back and gusset.
2. With wrong sides together, pin, then sew front and back to long edges for gusset. Trim seams to a scant 1/8". Apply binding to trimmed seam allowances.

Angel Log Cabin Hanging Towel

Fabrics & Supplies Needed for Towel Topper

All strips are cut across the fabric, selvage to selvage, assuming 42" of usable fabric.

- ❖ Towel topper pattern - on Sulky's website www.sulky.com
- ❖ 1 Terrycloth towel approximately 16" x 26" will make two topper towels
- ❖ 10" x 15" neutral fabric to embroider angel onto; trim to 6" x 7" after embroidery
- ❖ (2) 12" x 12" fabrics for topper front and backing   ❖ 12" x 12" batting for topper
- ❖ 2" x 10" strips of 4 light-to-dark fabrics (for diamond quilted version shown on page 124); or 1-3/4" x 10" strips of 6 light to dark fabrics (for log cabin version), (2) 2-1/2" x 10" dark strips and (1) 2-1/2" square for center of log cabin
- ❖ Fabric for trim band on bottom of towel, cut 3" x 18" or length needed
- ❖ 2 yds. of finished double-folded bias binding from a contrasting fabric
- ❖ Machine needle size: 14/90   ❖ Sulky KK 2000 Temporary Spray Adhesive
- ❖ Embroidery card - 43020 GNP Angels by Joyce Drexler for Great Notions
- ❖ Sulky Holoshimmer #6007 Gold   ❖ Sulky Stabilizers for embroidery
- ❖ Sulky 40 wt. Rayon #1263 Red Jubilee to match binding
- ❖ Sulky 12 wt. and 30 wt. Cotton Thread to match or contrast with band
- ❖ Sulky Bobbin Thread - for embroidery   ❖ General sewing supplies - see page 3

Embroider the Angel - See page 122 for instructions

Preparation of Towel and Trim Band

1. Fold the towel in half lengthwise and cut it in half.
2. Zig-zag, overcast or serge the cut edge to keep it from fraying.
3. On the 3" x 18" trim band fabric, press 1/4" under on all 4 sides. Press an additional 1" under on the 2 short sides.
4. To keep the trim band securely in place while stitching it to the towel, spray Sulky KK 2000 onto the wrong side of the band and smooth it onto the towel approximately 1-1/2" up from the bottom.
5. Lightly spray Sulky KK 2000 onto one strip of Sulky Solvy that is 2" larger than the applied band; smooth it over the top of the band. Spray a second piece of Solvy of similar size and smooth it onto the back side of the towel, even with the band. These two Solvy strips will ease in the band to the towel as well as help to keep the decorative stitching from sinking into the nap of the towel.
6. Thread the top with Sulky 12 wt. Cotton Blendables™ and put a matching Sulky 30 wt. Cotton Blendable in the bobbin.
7. Using a blanket stitch that is 3.0 mm long and 4.5 mm wide, stitch the band to the towel along the long edges of the band. Set the towel aside for now.

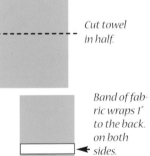

Cut towel in half.

Band of fabric wraps 1" to the back, on both sides.

Strip Piece Log Cabin Angel Applique (1/4 seam allowance)

Follow the instructions on previous page under Strip Piece Log Cabin Angel Applique, but use 1-1/2" strips instead. Miter and press corners of the strips.

Quilt Topper Fabric - Option 1

Prequilted Fabric ←

1. Lightly spray Sulky KK 2000 onto the 12" x 12" piece of batting.
2. Smooth one 12" x 12" fabric piece, wrong side down, over the batting.
3. Using a chalk marker, mark diagonal lines 1-1/2" apart in both directions, making a diamond grid.
4. Thread the top with Sulky Holoshimmer #6007 Gold and put Sulky Bobbin Thread in the bobbin.
5. Quilt all of the diagonal lines with a 3 mm long straight stitch.
6. Using the topper pattern from the Sulky website, cut out the 12" x 12" fabric that you just quilted and the 12" x 12" backing fabric. Set aside.

Apply the Block

1. Spray the wrong side of the log cabin applique with Sulky KK 2000 to hold it in place while stitching.
2. Find the lengthwise center of both the towel and the angel applique.
3. Place the bottom edge of the sprayed angel applique 1" above the trim band and smooth it in place, matching centers.
4. Using a featherstitch (2.5 mm length and 5.0 mm width) and the same Holoshimmer #6007 Gold, stitch over the seam lines of the log cabin.
5. Leave the folded edges of the log cabin strips free, creating a floating trim.

Option 2 - Angel on the Bottom

1. Follow the instructions for piecing the log cabin block on page 129. Note that the two outer side strips are wider (2-1/2") to accommodate the trapezoid shape of the topper. See illustration above right.

Construct the Towel Topper

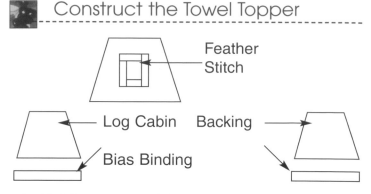

Feather Stitch

Log Cabin   Backing →

Bias Binding

1. Lightly spray KK 2000 on the wrong side of the backing and smooth it onto the batting. Repeat for the topper.
2. Apply the bias binding to this sandwich top and bottom.

Finishing

1. Hand baste the top of the towel.
2. Gather the top of the towel until its width equals the width of the bottom of the topper.
3. Insert 1" of the towel's top edge in between the topper and the backing. Pin in place.
4. Topstitch the towel in place by overstitching on the topstitching of the binding. Then stitch again on the bottom edge of the binding.

5. Cut two 20" lengths of bias binding for the side edges of the topper and ties.
6. At both ends of one bias binding strip, open up the ends and press a small hem to tuck in the corners. Re-press into the double-folded binding. Repeat for the second strip.
7. Apply these two strips to each side of the topper, encasing the raw edges of the bottom-bound bias. Continue stitching off the topper, closing up the bias for the ties.
8. Wrap it up for the perfect hostess gift.

Hand Soap Dispenser Cover

Fabrics & Supplies Needed for Soap Dispenser Cover

All strips are cut across the fabric, selvage to selvage, assuming 42˝ of usable fabric.

- ❖ Soap dispenser bottle - (we used a Softsoap 11.25 oz. bottle)
- ❖ Soap dispenser pattern - on the website: www.sulky.com
- ❖ Scraps of (8) 1-1/4" fabrics for log cabin strips and one 2" center square
- ❖ Muslin for lining
- ❖ 1 yd. of finished double-folded bias binding from a contrasting fabric
- ❖ Machine needle size: 14/90
- ❖ Sulky Soft 'n Sheer™ Stabilizer
- ❖ Sulky Holoshimmer #6007 Gold
- ❖ Sulky 40 wt. Rayon #1263 Red Jubilee to match binding
- ❖ Sulky Bobbin Thread
- ❖ Sewing thread for piecing
- ❖ Sulky KK 2000 Temporary Spray Adhesive
- ❖ General Sewing Supplies - see page 3

Preparation of Log Cabin Cover

From scraps of fabric, cut the following:

1. From a neutral fabric, cut one 2" square for the center.
2. Cut (1) 1-1/4" x 10" strip from 8 different fabrics.

Piecing the Log Cabin - use 1/4" seams

1. Sew strip 1 to the bottom edge of the 2" center square.
2. Trim strip 1 flush with the center square at both ends; press seam toward strip 1.
3. Add strip 2 to the left of the center square and strip 1.
4. Trim and press toward strip 2.
5. Continue to add strips 3, 4, 5, 6, 7, and 8 as above, trimming and pressing as with strips 1 and 2.

Decorative Quilting on Log Cabin Square

1. Cut 2 layers of Sulky Soft 'n Sheer, 1" larger than the finished log cabin block.
2. Spray Sulky KK 2000 on one layer of Sulky Soft 'n Sheer and smooth a second layer of Soft 'n Sheer onto it.
3. Lightly spray KK 2000 on the top of these 2 layers and smooth the log cabin block on top of it, right side up.
4. Thread the top with Sulky Holoshimmer #6007 Gold and put Sulky Bobbin Thread in the bobbin. See tips for using Metallic Threads on page 24.
5. Using a featherstitch (2.5 mm length and 4.0 mm width), quilt on top of all seam lines of the log cabin block. Set aside.

Make the Quilted Back Cover

1. From a fabric scrap, cut a 7" square.
2. Cut two 8" squares of Soft 'n Sheer.
3. Lightly spray Sulky KK 2000 onto one of the two Soft 'n Sheer squares and smooth the second one onto it.
4. Lightly spray KK 2000 on the top layer and smooth the fabric square, right side up, onto it.
5. Mark a diagonal line with chalk across this fabric square from corner to corner in either direction.
6. Thread the top with Sulky Holoshimmer #6007 Gold and put Sulky Bobbin Thread in the bobbin.
7. Channel quilt this chalked line using a 3.0 mm long straight stitch. Use the edge of a regular presser foot as a guide to channel quilt 1/2" away from both sides of the center line; continue quilting the remainder of the block at 1/2" intervals, or use a chalk marker to first draw all of the diagonal lines 1/2" apart. You could also use a quilting guide set at a 1/2" width. Set aside.

Cut Front and Back Covers

1. Using the pattern piece from the Sulky website: www.sulky.com, cut out the back cover.
2. When cutting out the front cover, find the center of the log cabin block and the center of the pattern piece; match and pin them together and cut it out.
3. Cut 2 linings from the muslin.
4. Using a scant 1/4" seam allowance, machine baste one lining to each front and back piece.
5. Set these 2 pieces aside.

Prepare Bias Binding

1. Cut the fabric for the binding into 1-1/2" bias strips. Stitch the cut strips together lengthwise.
2. Press the bias binding in half lengthwise to create double-folded binding.

Construct the Cover

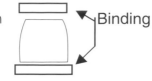

1. Thread the top and bobbin with Sulky 40 wt. Rayon #1263 Red Jubilee.
2. Apply the bias binding to the raw edges of both the front and the back cover at both the top and bottom.
3. Trim the binding even with the sides of the cover.
4. Using a 1/4" seam allowance, sew the side seams, **wrong** sides together, leaving the top and bottom edges open.
5. Slide the cover over the soap dispenser to check the fit. If needed, restitch to adjust for a snug fit.
6. Trim seams to a scant 1/8".
7. Apply the binding to the sides by folding a 1/2" to 3/4" tail of binding to the inside of the bottom before applying the binding up the first side, encompassing this folded tail when sewing. Near the top, stop with the needle down and cut a 1/2" to 3/4" tail of binding, folding the tail to the inside of the cover. Continue sewing.
8. Folding in the tails with this method will secure and hide the ends of the binding to the inside. Repeat on the other side of the cover.
9. Hand tack tail ends to the inside.

A Decorative Flower Pot Band

An ideal quick addition to that annual potted plant.
The Gift Angel is the perfect one for anytime giving!

Fabrics & Supplies Needed for Flower Pot Band

All strips are cut across the fabric, selvage to selvage, assuming 42" of usable fabric.

- ❖ Sewing machine with computerized applique/embroidery capability
- ❖ Flower pot band pattern on Sulky website: www.sulky.com
- ❖ Neutral fabric to embroider angel onto
- ❖ (1) 11" x 25" piece of fabric for band ❖ (1) 11" x 25" piece of muslin for backing
- ❖ (1) 11" x 25" piece of Warm and Natural™ Cotton Batting
- ❖ (2) 2" x 15" tie strips (from the same fabric as the band fabric)
- ❖ 2 yds. of finished double-folded bias binding from a contrasting fabric
- ❖ (1) 2" x 10" piece from each of 2 strips of scrap fabric (contrast to band fabric)
- ❖ Machine needle size: 14/90 ❖ Sulky KK 2000 Temporary Spray Adhesive
- ❖ Embroidery Card - #43020 GNP Angels by Joyce Drexler for Great Notions®
- ❖ Sulky Ultra Solvy™ Stabilizer for Embroidering Redwork Angels
- ❖ Sulky Totally Stable™ and Stiffy™ Stabilizers for Embroidering Filled Angels
- ❖ Sulky Holoshimmer #6007; Sulky 40 wt. Rayon #1263 to match Binding
- ❖ Sulky Bobbin Thread
- ❖ General Sewing Supplies - see page 3

Embroider the Angel - See page 122

Preparation of Quilted Band

1. Lightly spray Sulky KK 2000 onto the batting and smooth it onto the backing fabric.
2. Lightly spray KK 2000 on the top of the batting and smooth the wrong side of the fabric on top of it.
3. Using a chalk marker, draw diagonal lines 1-1/2" apart. (See previous page for directions or other options.)
4. Use a 3.0 mm straight stitch to quilt the drawn lines with Holoshimmer #6007 Gold on top and Sulky Bobbin Thread in the bobbin. See tips for using Metallic Threads on page 24.
5. Cut out the band using the pattern from the website: www.sulky.com.

Bias Binding Preparation

1. Cut fabric for binding into 2" bias strips. Stitch cut strips together lengthwise.
2. Fold and press bias binding lengthwise, wrong sides together, to create double-folded binding.

Angel Applique

1. Trim the angel block to 6" x 9".
2. Fold and press the (2) 2" x 10" strips in half lengthwise, wrong sides together, to form a trim; stitch one onto each side of the angel block. Find the center of the fabric band and the center of the angel block and pin in place, matching the centers.
3. Thread the top with Sulky Holoshimmer #6007 Gold and put Sulky Bobbin Thread in the bobbin. Featherstitch (2.5 mm length and 5.0 mm width) on the seam lines of the angel and the strips.
4. Continuing to use the featherstitch, stitch down both outside folds of the strips.
5. Machine baste the top and bottom of the angel and band a scant 1/4". Trim angel even with band.

Band Ties

1. Thread the top and bobbin with Sulky 40 wt. Rayon #1263 Red Jubilee.
2. Make the ties from the (2) 2" x 15" strips by folding each one in half lengthwise, right sides together; then, use a 1/4" seam allowance to seam all along one long end.
3. Using a turning tool or a safety pin, turn the ties right side out and press.
4. Find and mark the center of the band at the outer edges.
5. Sew the ties onto the band at the marked places.

Apply Binding

See page 131 for double-folded binding instructions.

1. Continue to use Sulky 40 wt. Rayon #1263 on the top and in the bobbin.
2. Start the binding at the bottom edge of the band. Leave the excess for seaming.
3. Apply the binding all around the band, leaving enough to overlap the beginning and ending pieces together.
4. Fold the ties over the binding and satin stitch them in place.

Holiday Quilted Potholder

✱ Fabrics & Supplies Needed for Quilted Potholder

All strips are cut across the fabric, selvage to selvage, assuming 42" of usable fabric.

- ❖ Sewing machine with computerized applique/embroidery capability
- ❖ Potholder and pocket pattern - on website: www.sulky.com
- ❖ Neutral fabric to embroider angel onto - cut large enough for hoop
- ❖ (2) 9" x 12" pieces of fabric for potholder
- ❖ (1) 9" x 12" piece of muslin for front pocket lining
- ❖ (2) 9" x 12" pieces of heat-resistant batting
- ❖ 1-1/2 yds. of finished double-folded bias binding from a contrasting fabric
- ❖ Machine needle size: 14/90   ❖ Sulky KK 2000 Temporary Spray Adhesive
- ❖ Embroidery card - #43020 GNP Angels by Joyce Drexler for Great Notions®
- ❖ Sulky Ultra Solvy™ Stabilizer for embroidering Redwork Angels
- ❖ Sulky Totally Stable™ and Stiffy™ Stabilizers for embroidering Filled Angels
- ❖ Sulky 30 wt. Cotton #1169 Bayberry Red and #1128 Dk. Ecru, or whatever matches your potholder fabric
- ❖ Sulky Bobbin Thread
- ❖ General Sewing Supplies - see page 3

✱ Embroider the Angel - See page 122.

✱ Quilting Main Potholder Pattern

1. Lightly spray KK 2000 onto one batting piece and smooth the second layer of batting over it.
2. Lightly spray KK 2000 onto the wrong side of the front fabric piece and smooth it over the layered batting. Repeat for the back piece.
3. Use a chalk marker to mark the front with diagonal lines 1-1/2" apart in both directions to form a diamond quilting pattern.
4. Set machine for a 3 mm long straight stitch. Quilt the diamond pattern using Sulky 30 wt. Cotton #1128 Dk. Ecru on the top and in the bobbin.
5. Using the main potholder pattern, cut out the quilted piece.

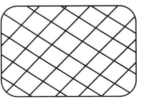

✱ Bias Binding Preparation

1. Cut fabric for binding into 2" bias strips. Stitch cut strips together lengthwise.
2. Press bias binding in half lengthwise, with wrong sides together, to create double-folded binding.

←Binding

←Angel Pocket

Prepare Angel Pocket

1. Using the pocket pattern, cut out the embroidered angel and the muslin lining.
2. Machine baste the angel pocket and the lining together.
3. Stitch the binding to the top edge of the pocket.
4. Baste the pocket to the potholder, leaving the top bound edge open.

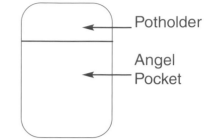

Attach Binding to Outer Edges

1. Find the top center of the potholder and mark it with a pin.
2. Start sewing the binding on the right side to the right of the pin that is marking the center point.
3. Sew the binding around the potholder. When you get back to the top, stitch over the beginning of the binding and off of the potholder.
4. Cut, leaving a 4" length, and stitch the binding together. Fold this tail to the back, forming a hanging loop. Use a zig-zag stitch with a 6 mm width and a 2.5 mm length to satin stitch the cut end.

Fabric Rag Bowl

Make a scrubbie holder

Fabrics & Supplies Needed for Fabric Rag Bowl

- ✤ Zig-zag sewing machine   ✤ Open-toe applique foot
- ✤ Nylon or cotton clothesline - 50 feet as packaged will give you a nice size bowl. *Note: Nylon is softer, which will result in a more flexible bowl. Cotton will produce a stiffer, firmer bowl.*
- ✤ Sulky 12 wt. and 30 wt. Cotton Blendables #4007 Red Brick, or your color of choice. For a subtle look, use the same color on both the top and bobbin, or mix them up for a different look inside and outside of the bowl.
- ✤ A variety of 3/4" to 1-1/2" wide fabric strips. It took only 8 strips - 20" long for the little scrubbie bowl. *(3/4" to 1" strips might be easier to use for the beginner.)* Tear the strips for a "thready" look. Rotary cut the strips for a smoother look.
- ✤ Size 16/100 or 18/110 topstitch or denim needle
- ✤ Spring-type wooden clothespin   ✤ General sewing supplies - see page 3

Set up the Machine

1. Thread the top with Sulky 12 wt. or 30 wt. Cotton Blendables #4007 Red Brick, and a matching or contrasting Sulky 30 wt. Cotton in the bobbin.
2. Insert a size 16/100 topstitch needle.
3. To show off the thread, set the machine for the longest and widest multiple zig-zag stitch or basic zig-zag stitch.

Bowl Construction

1. Begin by folding the end of the fabric strip over the raw edge of the clothesline.
2. Secure the end of the fabric strip to the clothesline with a pin, or spray the wrong side of the beginning end of the fabric strip with Sulky KK 2000 to secure it while you start the bowl bottom.
3. Start wrapping the fabric strip around the clothesline, over-lapping the fabric strip so that no clothesline shows.

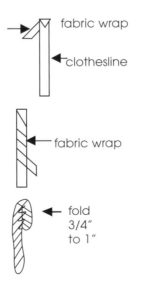

fabric wrap

clothesline

fabric wrap

fold 3/4" to 1"

Note: If an oval shaped bowl is desired, elongate the folded piece.

4. Fold over 3/4" to 1" of wrapped clothesline (see illustration below left), butting it up to the side of the already fabric-wrapped clothesline. Use a spring-type clothespin to act as a third hand to hold the end of the wrapped clothesline as you position the bowl under the presser foot.

5. Start zig-zagging at the top of the fold (this is the center bottom of the bowl). Keep the stitched clothesline to the left so the coil is flowing clockwise.

If you get started going the wrong way, just cut your threads, turn your piece over, and begin again.

6. Keep the wrapped clothesline centered under the presser foot so that the zig-zag stitch catches both sides of the coils.

7. Join the fabric strips by simply overlap-ping them onto one another as you continue to wrap the fabric strips snugly around the clothesline.

8. Continue stitching and turning in rounds while zig-zagging to catch both sides of the coil.
9. The bulk of the bowl will always be to the **left** of the needle.
10. Stitch around 3 times to make the flat bottom of the scrubbie bowl.
11. To form the sides of the bowl, turn it on edge, pressing the bowl against the bed of the machine; continue to wrap and stitch. (See photo on previous page.)
12. For the scrubbie bowl, keep turning and forming the sides of the bowl 10 rounds to make the height of the sides approximately 2-1/2".
13. To end, cut the clothesline at an angle and wrap the fabric strip around the cut end, and beyond it about 1".
14. Fold the 1" overlap back onto itself, then butt it up to the side; zig-zag it in place.

It's fun to add yarn, pieces of loose fabric, etc. as you wrap your bowl to make your bowl express your own creativeness.

Nancy Bryant

Katie Morris

Making Blendable Bowls at Abigayle's Quiltery in Ohio

Sewing with the girls! This is such fun and so addictive! No matter what your age …
you can do this!

You can add different coordinating strips for a scrappy bowl. You can make handles by simply extending a loop of wrapped clothesline as you stitch around the bowl. Nancy made her bowl really artsy by wrapping eyelash yarn along with the fabric strips. Make all sizes and shapes. They don't always have to be round. Oval bowls are nice too. You can shape the wrapped clothesline just about any way you want. Make placemats, coasters and rugs too! Make decorative bowls to match your quilts or other home decor. Even though we have been making these for over 25 years, they are still so much fun to make!

Sashed Squares Quilt

Block 1 Make 4

Block 2 Make 2

Block 3 Make 4

Block 4 Make 2

Credits:

Level: Beginner
Quilt designed by:
   Joyce Drexler and Nancy Bryant
Pieced by: Joyce Drexler
Quilted by: Evelyn Byler
   using Sulky 12 wt. Cotton
   Blendables #4020, #4013,
   #4030 and #4101.
Featured Fabric: Maywood Studio

Fabrics & Supplies Needed for Quilt:

*All strips are cut across the fabric, selvage to selvage,
assuming 42" of usable fabric. Cut off all selvages.
Make a Fabric Key - see page 8.*

❖ 3/4 yd. Fabric A - Center
❖ 1-1/2 yds. Fabric B - Narrow frame
❖ 1-1/4 yds. Fabric C - Wide frame
❖ 3-3/8 yds. Fabric D - Sashing & Border
❖ 5 yds. (42") or 2-1/2 yds. (108") for backing
❖ 3/4 yd. for binding
❖ Hobbs 80/20 Batting, at least 70" x 90"
❖ Sulky Cotton Blendables™ and Sulky
   Sliver™ Metallic
❖ Machine needle size: 14/90
❖ General sewing supplies - see page 3

Quilt Size: Approx. 64" x 84"
See other fabric versions
on pages 142, 143 and inside
back cover.

Cutting Instructions for non-directional fabrics

❖ Fabric A: Main Theme Fabric - Center
   Cut (3) 8-1/2" strips.

❖ Fabric B: Narrow Frame
   Cut (3) 3-1/2" strips.
   Cut (2) 11-1/2" strips.

❖ Fabric C: Wide Frame
   Cut (3) 4-1/2" strips.
   Cut (2) 12-1/2" strips.

❖ Fabric D: Corner, Sashing and Outer Border
   Corners: Cut (2) 4-1/2" strips.
             Cut (2) 3-1/2" strips.
   Sashing: Cut (12) 4-1/2" strips.
             From these, cut (12) 4-1/2" x 15-1/2"
             and (12) 4-1/2" x 19-1/2" strips.
   Outer Border: Cut (8) 4-1/2" strips.
                  From these, piece borders.

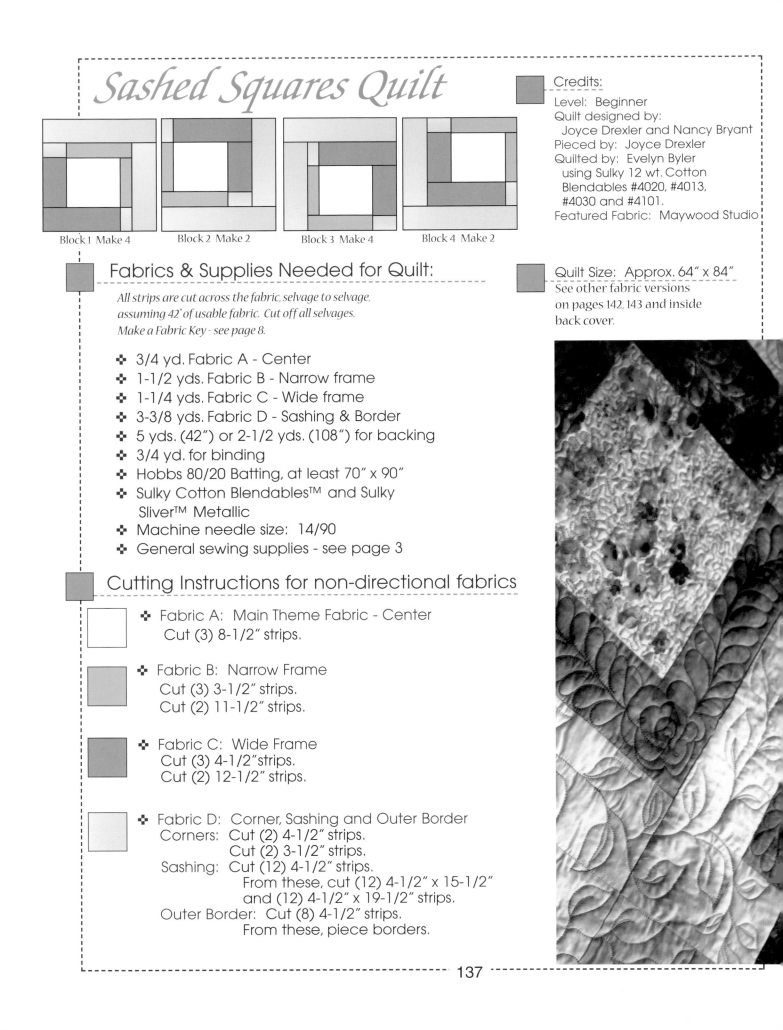

Interest is added to this simple design by turning the block before adding the sashing. It is a snap to strip piece if non-directional fabrics are used. If a directional motif fabric is selected for the center, use the traditional cutting instructions provided at the end of the pattern. Model - Carissa Noe, Joyce's granddaughter.

Strip Piecing Instructions - for Non-Directional Fabrics

Piece the Center Strip Set

1. Sew a 4-1/2" strip of Fabric C to an 8-1/2" strip of Fabric A and a 3-1/2" strip of Fabric B to make a 15-1/2" wide strip set. Press the seams toward the center strip. Make 3.

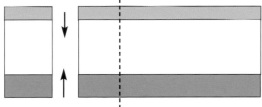

3-1/2" strip of Fabric B

8-1/2" strip of Fabric A

4-1/2" strip of Fabric C

Make 3 strip sets

2. Cut (12) 8-1/2" x 15-1/2" Unit "A".

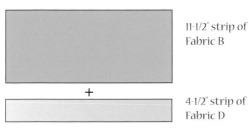

Cut 12 - Unit A

Piece the Top Strip Set

1. Sew an 11-1/2" strip of Fabric B to a 4-1/2" corner strip of Fabric D to make a 15-1/2" wide strip set. Press the seams toward Fabric D. Make 2.

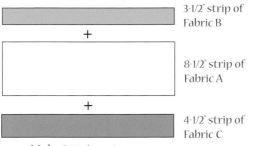

11-1/2" strip of Fabric B

4-1/2" strip of Fabric D

2. Cut (12) 3-1/2" x 15-1/2" Unit "B".

Cut 12 - Unit B

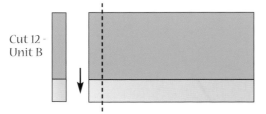

Piece the Bottom Strip Set

1. Sew a 12-1/2" strip of Fabric C to a 3-1/2" strip of Fabric D to make a 15-1/2" wide strip set. Press the seams toward Fabric D. Make 2.

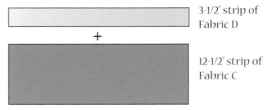

3-1/2" strip of Fabric D

12-1/2" strip of Fabric C

2. Cut (12) 4-1/2" x 15-1/2" Unit "C".

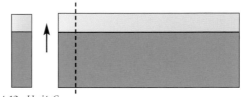

Cut 12   Unit C

Piece the Block

1. Sew the rows together as illustrated below to make the basic 15-1/2" square block. Make 12.

2. Press seams toward the center square.

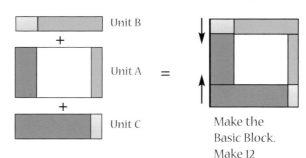

Unit B

Unit A =

Unit C

Make the Basic Block. Make 12

Add the Sashing Strips

Add sashing strips to the basic block to create four variations which are referred to as Block 1, Block 2, Block 3 and Block 4. The basic blocks are turned and the sashing strips are placed on different corners. Pay careful attention to these details when adding the sashing strips.

Block 1 (make 4)

1. Position the Basic Block as illustrated.

2. Add a 4-1/2" x 15-1/2" sashing strip to the right side. Press the seam toward the sashing strip.

3. Add a 4-1/2" x 19-1/2" sashing strip to the top. Press the seam toward the sashing strip.

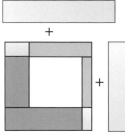

Make 4 - Block 1

Block 3 (make 4)

1. Position the basic block as illustrated.

2. Add a 4-1/2" x 15-1/2" sashing strip to the left side. Press the seam toward the sashing strip.

3. Add a 4-1/2" x 19-1/2" sashing strip to the top. Press the seam toward the sashing strip.

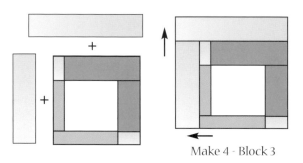

Make 4 - Block 3

Block 2 (make 2)

1. Turn and position the basic block as illustrated.

2. Add a 4-1/2" x 15-1/2" sashing strip to the right side. Press the seam toward the sashing strip.

3. Add a 4-1/2" x 19-1/2" sashing strip to the bottom. Press the seam toward the sashing strip.

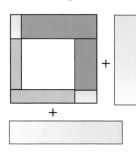

Make 2 - Block 2

Block 4 (make 2)

1. Turn and position the basic block as illustrated.

2. Add a 4-1/2" x 15-1/2" sashing strip to the left side. Press the seam toward the sashing strip.

3. Add a 4-1/2" x 19-1/2" sashing strip to the bottom. Press the seam toward the sashing strip.

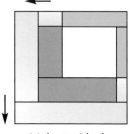

Make 2 - Block 4

Join the Blocks into Rows - (make 2)

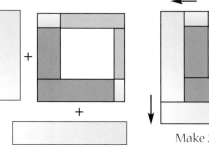

Block 1   Block 2   Block 1

1. Join a block 1 to opposite sides of a block 2. Make 2.

2. Press seams to the left.

These will be Rows 1 & 3.

140

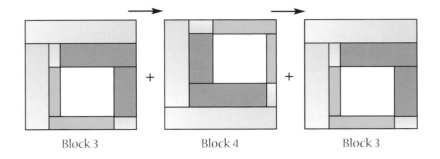

Block 3   Block 4   Block 3

1. Join a block 3 to opposite sides of a block 4, as illustrated. Make 2.

2. Press seams to the right.

These will be Rows 2 and 4.

Join the Rows to make the Quilt Top

1. Sew rows together as illustrated below to make the quilt top.

2. Press the seam allowances in opposite directions.

3. Add the 4-1/2" borders first to the sides, then to the top and bottom as illustrated below.

4. See page 28 for layering, backing, and batting. See page 30 for quilting directions.

Row 1
Block 1
Block 2
Block 1

Row 2
Block 3
Block 4
Block 3

Row 3
Block 1
Block 2
Block 1

Row 4
Block 3
Block 4
Block 3

Mountain Game

Another version of Sashed Squares Quilt
Finished size: 82" x 100"

Credits: Level: Intermediate using Directional Fabrics   Quilt pieced by: Carol Ingram
Quilted by: Evelyn Byler using Sulky 30 wt. Rayon #567 Butterfly Gold, #1001 White, and #1058 Tawny Brown. Sulky Holoshimmer #6011 Lt. Copper in ditches.
Featured Fabric: Hoffman Batiks. This quilt used directional center squares. Be careful when piecing directional fabrics so that a design doesn't end up upside down.
Carol added additional blocks and a border to make the quilt fit the queen-size bed.

Carol Ingram made this quilt for her husband, Bill. Photographed in a bedroom of their log cabin summer home in Franklin, NC. Carol painted and stenciled the walls herself.

Hand-dyed Leaves Another version of Sashed Squares Quilt

Credits: Level: Intermediate Quilt pieced by: Joyce Drexler Quilted by: Evelyn Byler using Sulky 12 wt. Cotton Blendables #4033 Grape Wine, #4019 Forest Floor and #4109 Jeweltones. Featured Fabric: Hand-dyed Fabrics This quilt used directional center squares. Be careful when piecing directional fabrics so that a design doesn't end up upside down. We also added two folded accent strips to the inside of the border.

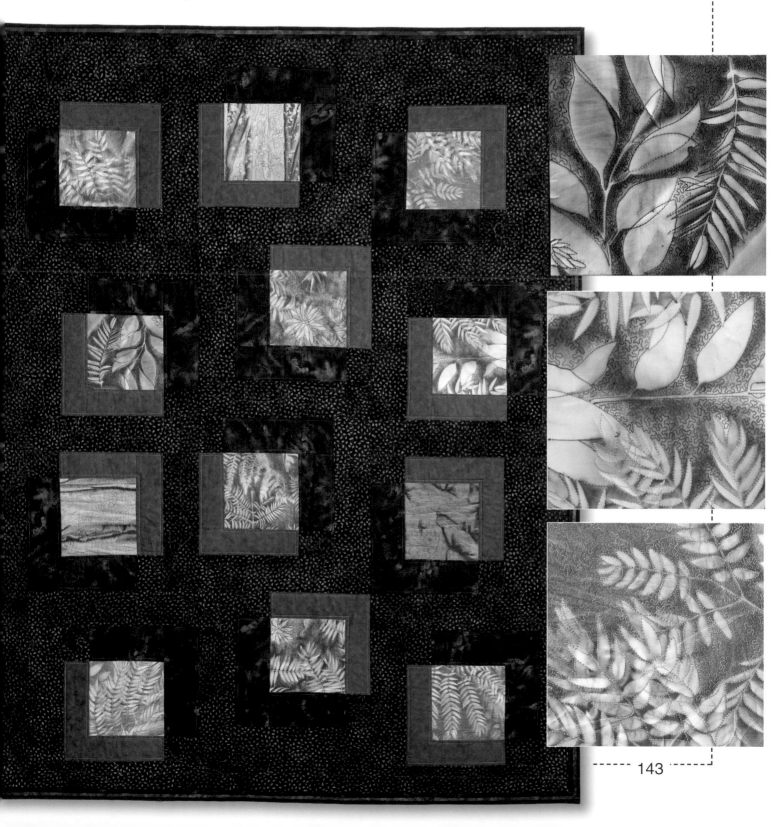

Cottage Flannel

Block 1
Make 17

Block 2
Fussy-cut 18
Theme Prints

Credits: Level: Beginner
Quilt designed and pieced by:
  Patti Lee (Inspired from pattern
  "Toastie Toes" by Lynette Jensen
Quilted by: Evelyn Byler
  using Sulky 30 wt. Solid Color
  Cotton Threads #1130 Dk. Brown
  and #1056 Med. Tawny Tan
Featured Flannel Fabric: Moda,
  and Thimbleberries by RJR

Fabrics & Supplies Needed for Quilt

All strips are cut across the fabric, selvage to selvage,
assuming 42" of usable fabric. Cut off all selvages.
Make a Fabric Key - Template is on page 8

- ❖ 2-1/4 yds. Fabric A - cottage theme print
- ❖ 1 yd. Fabric B - tan leaf print
- ❖ 1 yd. Fabric C - green print
- ❖ 3/4 yd. Fabric D - burgundy leaf print
- ❖ 1/2 yd. Fabric E - inner border
- ❖ 3/4 yd. binding
- ❖ 4-1/2 yds. (42") or 2-1/4 yds. (108") for backing
- ❖ Hobbs Heirloom Batting, at least 60" x 75"
- ❖ Sulky 30 wt. Cotton Threads and Sulky Polyester
    Invisible Thread - Smoke
- ❖ Machine needle size: 14/90
- ❖ General sewing supplies - see page 3

Cutting: Read page 5 before cutting.

- ❖ Fabric A: Theme Print
    Fussy Cut (18) 8-1/2" squares.

- ❖ Fabric B: Tan Leaf Print
    Cut (2) 4-1/2" strips.
    Cut (7) 2-1/2" strips.

- ❖ Fabric C: Green Print
    Cut (2) 4-1/2" strips.
    Cut (7) 2-1/2" strips.

- ❖ Fabric D: Burgundy Leaf Print
    Cut (9) 2-1/2" strips.
      From these, cut (34)
      2-1/2" x 8-1/2" strips.

- ❖ Fabric E: Inner Border
    Cut (6) 2-1/2" strips.

144

Quick and Easy Additional Projects:
- Fabric Rag Bowl
- Button Flange Throw Pillow

Quilt Size: Approx. 57" x 73"
See the same quilt using alternative fabric choices on page 148.

Fabric Rag Bowl p. 135.

Christmas Cats Pillow p. 147.

Close-up of Quilting

Make Block 1

1. Use a 1/4" seam allowance throughout. Sew (1) each of the 4-1/2" accent fabric strips together to form a 2-strip set. Press seams to the dark fabric. Make 2.

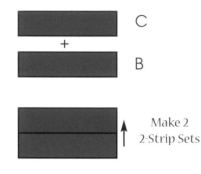

C
+
B

Make 2
2-Strip Sets

2. Cut the (2) 2-strip sets into (17) 4-1/2" x 8-1/2" Unit 1's.

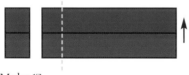

Make 17
Unit 1

3. Sew one Unit 1 and two 2-1/2" x 8-1/2" strips of Fabric D together to form Block 1. Make 17.

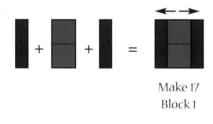

Make 17
Block 1

Sew the Blocks Together

1. Sew the blocks together using the 18 Fabric A squares and the 17 Block 1's, turning all of the block 1's as illustrated in the diagram in the next column. Press seams toward the Fabric A squares. Make 7 rows.

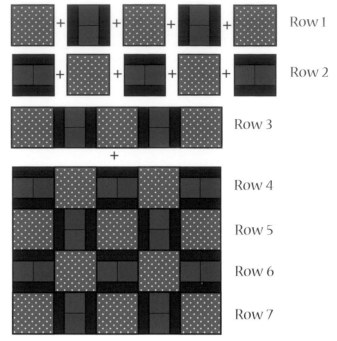

Row 1

Row 2

Row 3

+

Row 4

Row 5

Row 6

Row 7

2. To create the quilt top, sew the rows to one another, nesting seams. Press. The top should now measure 40-1/2" x 56-1/2".

Sew on the Inner Borders

Since the yardage is based on a crosswise cut, measure and pin carefully to prevent stretching. Join the 42" strips diagonally, if needed. See page 26 for details.

Sew the Checkered Outer Border

1. Sew the 2-1/2" strips of Fabrics B and C together to form 7 strip sets. Press the seams to the dark fabric.

C
+
B
=
Make 7 Strip Sets

2. Cut the (7) strip sets into (112) 2-1/2" x 4-1/2" Unit 2's.

Make 112
Unit 2

3. Sew all but 8 of these Unit 2's together to form (52) 4-1/2" four-patch blocks. Sew the blocks into strips to make the checkered outer border. Use the remaining (8) Unit 2's to alternate the outer border pattern. Press to one side.

+

=

Make 52

146

Cottage Flannel Buttoned-Flanged Pillow

Use a 1/4" seam allowance throughout.

Fabrics & Supplies for Pillow

- ❖ Fabric A - 8-1/2" square Cottage print
- ❖ Fabric B - 12-1/2" square Tan leaf print for pillow back
- ❖ Fabric C - 2-1/4" x 42" Green print
- ❖ Fabric D - (4) 8-1/2" x 12-1/2" strips Burgundy leaf print
- ❖ 12" pillow form ❖ Chalk Marker
- ❖ 12-1/2" square of cotton batting
- ❖ Sulky KK 2000 Temporary Spray Adhesive
- ❖ (4) 3-1/2" x 12-1/2" strips of Sulky Cut-Away Plus Stabilizer
- ❖ Sulky 12 wt. & 30 wt. Cotton Threads #1056 Med. Tawny Tan, and Sulky Smoke Invisible Thread
- ❖ (6) 3/4" buttons
- ❖ Machine needle size: 14/90
- ❖ General sewing supplies - see page 3

Piece and Quilt Pillowtop

1. Sew a 2-1/4" strip of fabric C onto all four sides of Fabric A. We "fussy cut" this fabric scene to highlight the cottage scene of our choice.
2. Spray Sulky KK 2000 onto the back of the pieced pillow top and smooth it over the batting.
3. Thread the top and bobbin with Sulky Polyester Invisible Thread. Using either a free-motion or machine-fed straight stitch, stitch in the ditch around all four sides of the cottage print and around the cottage and barns.
4. With Sulky 12 wt. Cotton #1056 Med. Tawny Tan on top and a matching 30 wt. Cotton in the bobbin, stipple stitch the green border area.

Pillow Hems and Finishing

1. Fold the (4) 8-1/2" x 12-1/2" Fabric D strips in half lengthwise, wrong sides together, and press. Open each piece and lightly spray the wrong side with KK 2000.

2. To give body and stability to the hems and keep them from getting limp over time, lay one 3-1/2" x 12-1/2" strip of Sulky Cut-Away Plus on the bottom half of each of the sprayed pieces. Fold over (wrong sides together) and smooth away any creases. Set two aside.

3. With your cottage right side up lengthwise, stitch one of the other two to each side of the pillow top.

4. Approximately 1" from the hem edge, stitch 3 buttonholes on each of these two hem pieces, 2" in from each side and the third in the center of the hem. Cut buttonholes open.

5. Stitch the remaining two hem pieces to the 12-1/2" square of Fabric B.

6. Place pillow top together with pillow back, right sides together, matching seams and edges. Stitch both long edges. Turn right side out and press.

7. On the inside of the bottom hem pieces, use a chalk marker to mark through buttonholes for button placement. Sew on buttons with Sulky 12 wt. Cotton #1056 Med. Tawny Tan.

Christmas Cats
Another version of Cottage Flannel.

Credits: Level: Beginner   Quilt designed and pieced by: Patti Lee   Quilted by: Evelyn Byler using Sulky 30 wt. Rayon Thread #2208   Featured Fabric: Benartex & Moda

Fussy-Cut Theme Fabric --- Look for prints that express your interests,
and make this quick and easy quilt this weekend!

Stars in my Eyes

Let the light shine on as it twinkles in your eyes. You will be the ultimate star when you make this quilt and give it away.

Stars in My Eyes

Fabrics & Supplies Needed for Quilt:

All strips are cut across the fabric, selvage to selvage, assuming 42" of usable fabric. Use 1/4" seam allowance.

- Fabric A: 5 yds. light yellow fabric
- Fabric B: 1-1/2 yds. blue hydrangea fabric which includes yardage for binding
- Fabric C: 1-1/4 yds. dark blue fabric
- Fabric D: 3/4 yd. light blue fabric
- Backing: 6 yds. (42") or 2-1/2 yds. (108")
- Batting, at least 76" x 100"
- Sulky 12 wt. Cotton Blendables™ #4002 Buttercream
- Machine needle size: 14/90 Topstitch
- General sewing supplies - See page 3

Credits:
Level: Intermediate
Quilt designed by: Nancy Bryant
Pieced by: Beverly Morris
Quilted by: Evelyn Byler using Sulky Blendable #4002 Buttercream
Featured Fabric:
    Hydrangeas by Lakehouse

Quilt Size: Approx. 65-1/2" x 81"

See the other color way versions: below, page 155, and on the front cover.

The Echo Quilting around each star makes them stand out, while the Meander Quilting makes the background recede.

Cutting: Read page 5 before cutting.

Make a Fabric Key - page 8.

All cutting measurements include 1/4" wide seam allowances.

- Fabric A: Yellow
    Cut (4) 6-1/2" strips. From these, cut (19) 6-1/2" squares.
    Cut (6) 5-1/2" strips. From these, cut (42) 5-1/2" squares.
    Cut (6) 4-1/2" strips. From these, cut (47) 4-1/2" squares.
    Cut (7) 3-1/2" strips. From these, cut (7) 3-1/2" x 15-1/2" strips and (7) 3-1/2" x 12-1/2" strips.
    Cut (5) 3-1/2" strips. From these cut (54) 3-1/2" squares.
        Cut (8) 3-1/2" strips for the borders.

- Fabric B: Blue Hydrangea
    Cut (3) 6-1/2" strips. From these, cut (14) 6-1/2" squares.
    Cut (2) 5-1/2" strips. From these, cut (12) 5-1/2" squares.
    Cut (1) 4-1/2" strip. From this, cut (9) 4-1/2" squares.

- Fabric C: Dark Blue
    Cut (2) 6-1/2" strips. From these, cut (7) 6-1/2" squares.
    Cut (2) 5-1/2" strips. From these, cut (12) 5-1/2" squares.
    Cut (2) 4-1/2" strips. From these, cut (18) 4-1/2" squares.

- Fabric D: Light Blue Dot
    Cut (2) 5-1/2" strips. From these, cut (10) 5-1/2" squares.
    Cut (1) 4-1/2" strip. From this, cut (9) 4-1/2" squares.

150

Make Triangles - Read page 9.

1. Mark or press a diagonal line from corner to corner on the wrong side of (7) 6-1/2" yellow squares of Fabric A.

2. Layer each one, right sides together, with a 6-1/2" dk. blue square of Fabric C.

3. Stitch 1/4" away from each side of the solid line. Cut apart along the solid diagonal line. Press seams to the dark. Make 14.

Make 14

4. Mark or press a diagonal line from corner to corner on the wrong side of the (7) 6-1/2" blue hydrangea squares of Fabric B.

5. Layer each one, right sides together, with a 6-1/2" dk. blue square of Fabric C.

6. Stitch 1/4" away from each side of the solid line. Cut apart along the solid diagonal line. Press to the dark. Make 14.

7. Mark or press a diagonal line *across the sewn seam* on the wrong side of each of the 14 dark blue/yellow half-square triangle units.

8. Layer each one, right sides together, with a dark blue/blue hydrangea half-square triangle unit.

9. Stitch 1/4" away from each side of the solid line. Cut apart along the solid diagonal line. Press to the dark and trim the quarter-square triangle squares to measure 5-1/2".

Make 28

Assemble Block 1 - Large Star

1. Sew the 5-1/2" quarter-square triangle squares to the 5-1/2" Fabric A yellow background squares as illustrated below.

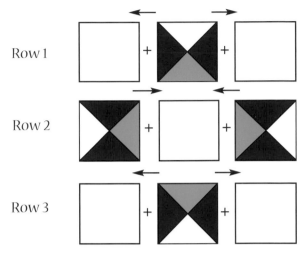

Row 1

Row 2

Row 3

2. Press toward the unpieced squares.

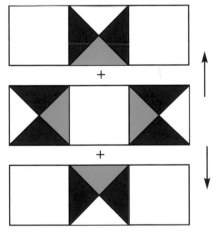

3. Sew the rows together. Press seams toward the outer sections. Make 7. Set them aside.

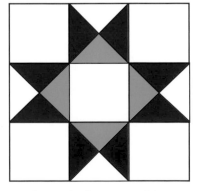

Make 7 Block 1 - 15-1/2" Square

Make Triangles for Block 2

1. Mark or press a diagonal line from corner to corner on the wrong side of (7) 5-1/2" squares of yellow fabric A.

2. Layer them, right sides together, with one each of (4) 5-1/2" squares of light blue fabric D; layer (3) of them with a 5-1/2" square of blue hydrangea fabric B.

3. Stitch 1/4" away from each side of the solid line. Cut apart along the solid diagonal line to make 8 light blue/yellow and 6 yellow/blue hydrangea half-square triangle units. Press to the dark fabric.

Make 8

4. Mark or press a diagonal line from corner to corner on the wrong side of the remaining (4) 5-1/2" light blue squares of fabric D. Layer each one, right sides together, with a 5-1/2" blue hydrangea square of fabric B.

Make 6

5. Stitch 1/4" away from each side of the solid line. Cut apart along the solid diagonal line. Press (6) units to the blue hydrangea. Press the rest to the light blue. Make 8.

6. Mark or press a diagonal line on the wrong side of each of the (8) light blue/yellow units.

Make 8

7. Layer a light blue/yellow unit, right sides together, on top of a blue hydrangea/light blue unit that is pressed to the light blue.

Make 16

8. Stitch 1/4" from each side of the solid line. Cut apart along the solid line. Press to the dark and trim the quarter-square triangle squares to measure 4-1/2". Make 16.

9. Mark or press a diagonal line on the wrong side of each of the (6) yellow/blue hydrangea squares.

10. With right sides together, layer a yellow/blue hydrangea unit on top of a light blue/blue hydrangea unit that is pressed to the blue hydrangea.

11. Stitch 1/4" from each side of the solid line. Cut apart along the solid line. Press to the dark and trim the quarter-square triangle squares to measure 4-1/2".

Make 12

Make Blocks 2A and 2B

1. Using the (28) 4-1/2" quarter-square triangles and (35) 4-1/2" squares of fabric A, assemble a total of (7) 12-1/2" square blocks, (4) with light blue points (Block 2A) and (3) with blue hydrangea points (Block 2B).

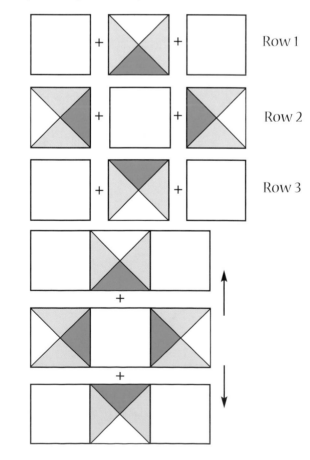

Row 1

Row 2

Row 3

2. Sew a 3-1/2" x 12-1/2" strip of fabric A to the left side of each of the (7) star blocks.

3. Sew a 3-1/2" x 15-1/2" strip to the bottom of each of the (7) star blocks.

4. All (4) Block 2A and (3) Block 2B blocks should now measure 15-1/2" square.

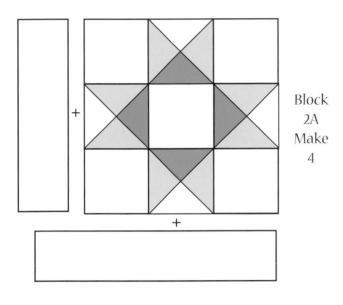

Block
2A
Make
4

5. Set them aside for now.

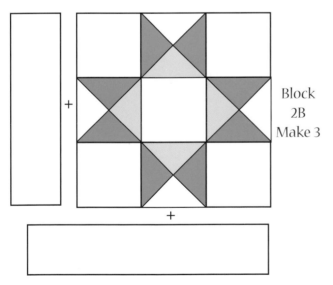

Block
2B
Make 3

Make Triangles for Block 3

1. Mark or press a diagonal line from corner to corner on the wrong side of (12) 4-1/2" yellow squares of fabric A.

2. Layer one each of (6) of them, right sides together, with one each of (6) 4-1/2" fabric D squares. Layer (3) of them with a 4-1/2" dark blue square of fabric C. Layer the remaining (3) with a 4-1/2" blue hydrangea square of fabric B.

3. Stitch 1/4" away from each side of the solid line. Cut apart along the solid, diagonal line. Press to the dark fabrics.

Make 12   Make 6   Make 6

4. Mark or press a diagonal line from corner to corner on the wrong side of (12) light blue 4-1/2" squares of fabric D.

5. Layer one each of (6) of them, right sides together, with one each of (6) 4-1/2" squares of blue hydrangea fabric B. Layer the other 6 with the 4-1/2" dark blue squares of fabric C.

6. Stitch 1/4" away from each side of the solid line. Cut apart along the solid diagonal line. Press toward the light blue.

7. Mark or press a diagonal line on the wrong side of all of the half-square triangle squares that have yellow in them.

8. Layer the dark blue/yellow units on top of the dark blue/light blue units, right sides together.

9. Layer the blue hydrangea/yellow units on top of the blue hydrangea/light blue units, right sides together.

10. Layer half of the light blue/yellow units on top of the light blue/blue-hydrangea units, right sides together.

11. Layer the other half of the light blue/yellow units on top of the light blue/dark blue units, right sides together.

12. Stitch 1/4" away from each side of the solid line. Cut apart along the solid diagonal line. Press to the dark.

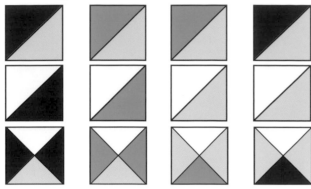

13. Trim quarter-square triangle squares to measure 3-1/2". Make 12 of each for a total of 48.

 ## Sew Blocks 3A and 3B

1. Using the (48) 3-1/2" quarter-square triangles, (54) 3-1/2" squares of fabric A, and (12) 6-1/2" squares of fabric A, assemble a total of (6) 15-1/2" blocks, 3 darks (Block 3A) and 3 lights (Block 3B).

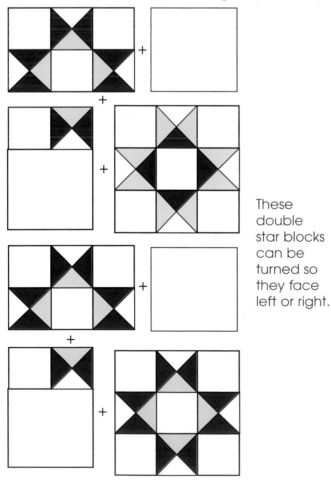

These double star blocks can be turned so they face left or right.

 ## The Blocks We Have Made

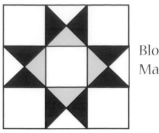

Block 1
Made 7

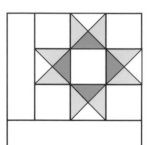 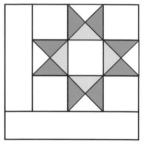

Block 2A Made 4   Block 2B Made 3

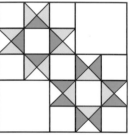

Block 3A Made 3   Block 3B Made 3

You should arrange the blocks in your quilt the way you think it looks the best. We assembled our Blue and Yellow Stars in My Eyes Quilt as follows:

Row 1	2A	1	3BR	2B
Row 2	1	3BL	2A	1
Row 3	3AR	2B	1	3AL
Row 4	2A	1	3BR	2B
Row 5	1	3AL	2B	1

R = angle stars to the right
L = angle stars to the left

Horizontal Borders

If necessary, join the (8) 3-1/2" x 42" border strips diagonally. Read pages 26-36 for finishing.

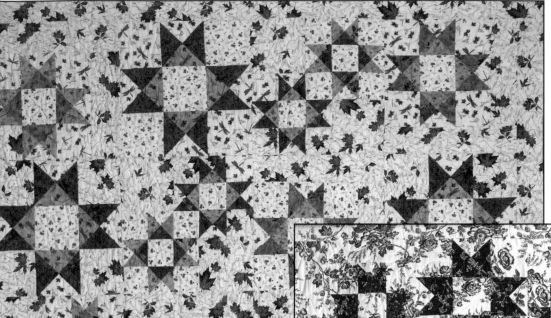

Other color-ways of the quilt "Stars in my Eyes". To the left, "Fall Stars", uses a printed background flannel fabric which gives the quilt a busier look, making the star blocks less dominant.

Credits:
Level: Intermediate
Quilt designed by: Nancy Bryant
Quilted by: Abigayle's Quiltery
    using an all-over leaf design
    with Sulky 30 wt. Cotton
    Blendables #4103 Pansies.
Featured Fabric: Moda Flannel

Credits:
Level: Intermediate
Quilt designed by: Nancy Bryant
Quilted by: Rose-Marie Newcomb
    using an all-over star design
    with Sulky 12 wt. White Cotton
Featured Fabric: Various Manufacturer's

Stars in My Eyes Corded Pillow

Fabrics & Supplies for Star Pillow

All strips are cut across the fabric, selvage to selvage, assuming 42" of usable fabric. Use 1/4" seam allowance. Cut off all selvages.

- Fabric: See "Cutting" below
- Batting - 16" square
- Sulky Soft 'n Sheer Stabilizer - 16" square
- Sulky KK 2000 Temporary Spray Adhesive
- 15" Pillow Form
- 85" of Cording
- Sulky 12 wt. Cotton Blendables™ #4002 Buttercream
- Machine needle size: 14/90 Topstitch
- General sewing supplies - See page 3

Cutting:

All cutting measurements include 1/4" wide seam allowances. Make a Fabric Key substituting your fabric choices. Page 8.

- Fabric A: Light Yellow - Background/Stars
  Cut (5) 5-1/2" squares.
  Cut (1) 6-1/2" square.
  Cut (2) 1-3/4" x 42" strips for borders.
    Cut (2) 15-1/2" x 40" rectangles for slip cover back.

- Fabric B: Light Fabric
  Cut (1) 6-1/2" square.

- Fabric C: Dark Blue Triangles
  Cut (2) 6-1/2" squares.

- Fabric D: Light Blue Hydrangea Triangles
  Cut (2) 1-1/2" x 42" cording strips.

Make the Cording: See page 56.

1. Piece the 1-1/2" fabric strips together at the ends to make a length of fabric approximately 84" long. Fold and press the strip lengthwise, wrong sides together, matching the raw edges.

2. Lay the cord on the inside of the folded strip and use a cording foot or zipper foot to stitch a straight stitch close to the cording.

Assemble the Pillow:

1. Follow the directions for making a 15-1/2" Star Block 1, page 151.

2. Once the pillow top is pieced, make a "quilt sandwich" by spraying KK 2000 onto the 16" square of batting and smoothing the 16" square of Sulky Soft 'n Sheer Stabilizer over it; turn it over. Spray KK 2000 onto the wrong side of the pillow top and smooth the pillow top over the batting.

3. Quilt the "quilt sandwich" as desired using Sulky 12 wt. Cotton Blendables #4002 Buttercream, or a color of your choice.

4. Attach the cording as shown on page 56.

5. Make the slip cover back using the (2) 15-1/2" x 40" light yellow fabric rectangles. See page 55 for details.

Scrappy Bear Paws

 Credits:

Level: Intermediate
Designed by:
    Nancy Bryant
Quilt pieced by:
    Beverly Morris
Quilted by: Evelyn Byler
    using Sulky 30 wt.
    Cotton Thread
Featured Fabric:
    Hoffman Batiks

Close-up of Quilting

Scrappy Bear Paw Placemat

Make a block as described on the following pages. Add a 2" strip of dark batik and then another 2" strip of light to widen the square into a rectangle. Layer, quilt and bind in the same manner as you would a full-size quilt.

157

Scrappy Bear Paws

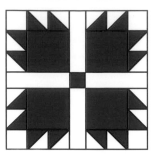

Make 12 - 11" Blocks

Credits:
Level: Intermediate
Quilt designed by:
 Nancy Bryant
Pieced by: Joyce Drexler
Hand Quilted by:
 Abigayle's Quiltery
  using Sulky 30 wt.
  Blendables
Featured Fabrics:
 Scrappy Mix

Fabrics & Supplies Needed for Quilt:

Cut out some pieces from each of at least 10 to 12 fabrics to distribute the patterns and colors throughout the quilt. All strips are cut across the fabric, selvage to selvage, assuming 42" of usable fabric. Cut off all selvages.
Make a Fabric Key - see page 8.

* Dark fabrics - 4-1/2 yds. of assorted darks
   Set aside a 1 yard piece for binding
* Light fabrics - 4-1/2 yds. of assorted white on
   white or cream on cream for backgrounds
* 5 yds. (42") or 2-1/4 yds. (108") for backing
* Hobbs Heirloom Batting, at least 60" x 75"
* Sulky 30 wt. Cotton Thread #1001 Bright White
   for piecing & quilting
* *If quilting by machine - use needle size: 14/90*
* *If quilting by hand - see page 35*
* General sewing supplies - see page 3

Quilt Size:
Approx. 56" x 71"

Quick & Easy Home
Decorating Project:

* Tablerunner - p.164
   by Beverly Morris
* Pillow - p.164
   by Beverly Morris
* Placemat - p.157
   by Beverly Morris

See a different
color version
of this quilt
on page 157.

Cutting: Read page 5 before cutting.

* Dark Fabrics A:
   Set aside a one yard piece for binding.
   Cut the following from remaining dark fabrics:
   (31) 2" x 11" strips   (112) 2" squares
   (96) 2-1/2" squares   (48) 3-1/2" squares
   (4) 5" squares   (42) 3" x 5" strips
   (8) 3-3/8" squares

* Light Fabrics B:
   Cut the following from light fabrics:
   (62) 2" x 11" strips   (128) 2" squares
   (48) 2" x 5" strips   (96) 2-1/2" squares
   (8) 3-3/8" squares   (42) 3" x 5" strips

Make the Triangles

Refer to page 10 for methods of making Half-Square Triangles - Option 2.

1. You will need (96) 2-1/2" dark squares and (96) 2-1/2" light squares to make 192 half-square triangles.

2. Once the 192 half-square triangles are made and pressed, trim each pieced square to precisely 2" x 2".

Assemble the Blocks

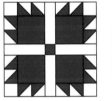

Make 12 - 11" Square Blocks

Pieces Needed:
(192) half-square triangles
  (48) 2" x 5" light strips
  (48) 2" light squares for corners
  (12) 2" dark squares for centers
  (48) 3-1/2" dark squares for paws

1. Join the half-square triangles in pairs, *half facing toward the left, half facing toward the right.* Press the seams toward the dark, or in the direction of the arrows.

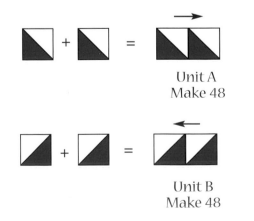

Unit A
Make 48

Unit B
Make 48

---

2. Sew a 2" light square to the left side of a Unit A, making a Unit C. Press toward the square. Make 48.

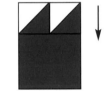

Unit C - Make 48

3. Sew a Unit B to the top of a 3-1/2" dark square, making a Unit D. Press seam toward square. Make 48.

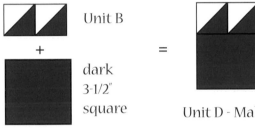

Unit B

+

dark 3-1/2" square

Unit D - Make 48

4. Sew a Unit C to the right side of a Unit D to make a Unit E. Press. Unit should measure 5" square. Make 48.

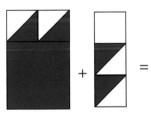

Unit D   Unit C   Unit E - Make 48

5. Sew a Unit E to a 2" x 5" light strip to make a Unit F. Press. Make 24.

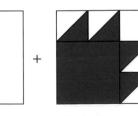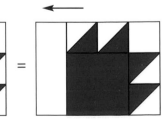

Unit E   Unit F - Make 24

6. Rotate a Unit E 1/4 turn to the left and sew it to a Unit F to make a Unit G. Press. Make 24.

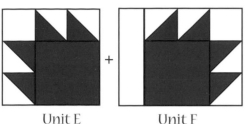

Unit E   Unit F

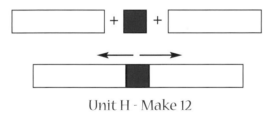

Unit G - Make 24

7. Sew a 2" x 5" light strip to both sides of a 2" dark square to make a Unit H. Press toward the light strips. Make 12.

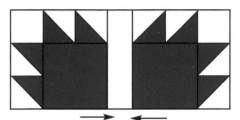

Unit H - Make 12

8. Sew a Unit H to the bottom of a Unit G. Then turn a Unit G one half turn and sew it onto the bottom as illustrated below to make an 11" square Bear Paw Block. Make 12.

Make 12 Bear Paw Blocks

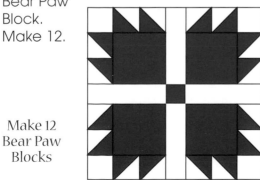

Make Cornerstones

Pieces Needed:
(100) 2" dark squares
(80) 2" light squares

1. Sew 40 segments like those below. Press toward the dark.

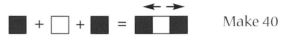

Make 40

2. Sew 20 segments like those below. Press toward the dark.

Make 20

3. Assemble 20 nine-patch blocks following the illustration below. These blocks should measure 5" square. Press. Make 20.

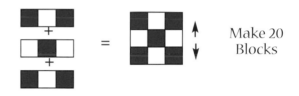

Make 20 Blocks

Sashing Strips and Assembly

Pieces Needed:
(31) 2" x 11" dark strips
(62) 2" x 11" light strips

1. Sew a dark strip to a light strip. Make 31 units.
2. Add a light strip to the dark side of all 31 units.

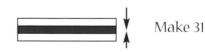

Make 31

3. Press the seam allowances toward the dark strip.
4. The individual sashing units are now complete and each should measure 5" x 11".
5. Assemble 5 rows consisting of 3 sashing units joining 4 nine-patch cornerstones as shown on the next page. Press seam allowances toward the sashing as indicated by the arrows.

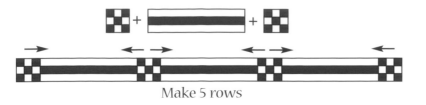

Make 5 rows

6. Join sashing units to 3 Bear Paw Blocks as shown below. Press seam allowances toward the sashing as indicated by the arrows. Make 4 rows.

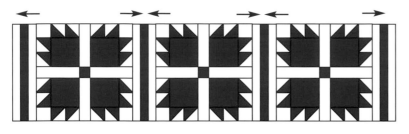

7. Join the completed Bear Paw Block rows with sashing unit rows as indicated below until you have a total of 4 blocks down and 3 across.

Make Triangles for Borders

Pieces Needed:
- (42) 3" x 5" light strips
- (42) 3" x 5" dark strips

- (8) 3-3/8" dark squares
- (8) 3-3/8" light squares

- (4) 5" dark squares

Make 16 Half-Square Triangles
(See Option 2 page 10.)

1. On the wrong side of the 3-3/8" ligh squares, draw a diagonal line from corner to corner.

2. Layer a 3-3/8" dark square and a 3-3/8" light square, right sides together.

3. Stitch 1/4" away from each side of the drawn line.

4. Cut apart on the drawn line.

5. Unfold and press seam allowances toward the dark fabric.

6. Trim each square to measure 2-3/4 Make 16 half-square triangles.

7. Join the half-square triangles into 8 sets of two as illustrated below.

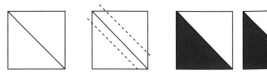

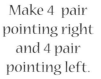 

Make 4 pair
pointing right
and 4 pair
pointing left.

Make Pieced Borders

1. Sew the 3" x 5" dark strips to the 3" x 5" light strips in pairs.

2. Sew the sides of the pairs together into a strip nine pairs wide (9 light, 9 dark). Make two units.

3. Add a triangle unit to each end, facing as illustrated.

4. To make the top and bottom borders, add a dark 5" square to both ends.

5. Make two units, twelve pairs wide (12 light, 12 dark).

6. To make the side borders, add a triangle unit to each end, facing as illustrated below.

Add the Outer Borders

1. Measure the sides of the quilt top along both edges, then through the center. All 3 should be equal. If not, refer to "Adjusting the Outer Borders" section below.

2. Add the pieced side borders to make the corner Bear Paw correctly. The left border must have a red strip at the top. The right side must have a white strip at the top.

3. Measure the top and bottom along both edges, then through the center. All 3 should be equal. If not, refer to "Adjusting the Outer Borders" section below.

4. Add the pieced top and bottom borders. The top must have a white strip on the left. The bottom must have a white strip at the right corner.

Adjusting the Outer Borders

The following simple technique allows us to adjust the fit of a pieced border to compensate for any size variance in the piecing. Take in or let out several seams 1/8" each until the correct size is achieved. Each 1/8" adjustment will shorten or lengthen the border by 1/4", as the seam affects both fabrics. This slight difference is usually not visible and enables us to achieve the correct fit.

Layering - See p. 28

Layering - See p. 28

Hand Quilting - See p. 35

Hand Quilting - See p. 35

This quilt was hand quilted using both Sulky solid white 12 wt. cotton and Sulky Blendable #4001 Parchment.

Machine Quilting - See p. 30

Machine Quilting - See p. 30

Binding - See p. 46-47

Binding - See p. 46-47

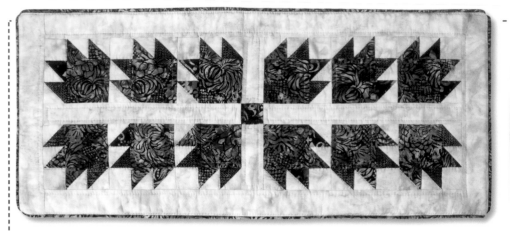

Scrappy Bear Paw Pillow & Tablerunner

Hand quilted with
Sulky 30 wt. Cotton

Fabrics & Supplies for Pillow

Since this is a scrappy pillow,
try to cut out some pieces from
each of at least 10 to 12 fabrics to distribute the
patterns and colors throughout the pillow. All strips are
cut across the fabric, selvage to selvage,
assuming 42" of usable fabric. Cut off all selvages.

- Dark Fabrics - Total 1/2 yd. assort. darks
- Light Fabrics - Total 1/2 yd. assort. lights
- 1/2 yd. for binding
- 22" square for backing
- 2 pieces 22" x 26" for Pillow Backing
     Slip-covers - see page 54
- Hobbs Batting, at least 24" square
- 20" Pillow Form
- Sulky 30 wt. Cotton Thread #1001
     Bright White for piecing and quilting
- *If quilting by machine, use a 14/90 needle.*
- *If quilting by hand, see page 35.*
- General sewing supplies - see page 3

Fabrics for Tablerunner

- Dark Fabrics - Total 1/2 yd. assort. darks
- Light Fabrics - Total 2/3 yd. assort. lights
- Backing & Batting - 15" x 52"
- Binding - 1/3 yard
- General sewing supplies - see page 3

Cutting for Pillows:

 ❖ Dark Fabrics A:

Cut the following from dark fabrics:
   (8) 2-1/2" squares
  (21) 2" squares
   (4) 3-1/2" squares
   (4) 2" x 11" strips

 ❖ Light Fabrics B:

Cut the following from light fabrics:
   (8) 2" x 11" strips
  (20) 2" squares
   (4) 2" x 5" strips
   (8) 2-1/2" squares

Credits:

Level: Intermediate
Bear Paw Pillow & Tablerunner
Designed by: Beverly Morris
Pieced by: Beverly Morris
Hand Quilted by: Abigayle's using
     Sulky 30 wt. Cotton
Featured Fabrics: Use a variety of
     reds and white-on-whites, or a
     variety of blues and white-on-
     whites from various manufacturers.

Make 16 Half-Square Triangles

1. Use (8) 2-1/2" dark squares and (8) 2-1/2" light squares to make 16 half-square triangles, following the instructions on page 9 for the method you prefer for making half-square triangles. Press.

2. Trim each square to precisely 2" x 2".

Make the Block

Make 1 - 11" square block

Follow the instructions on pages 160-161 to make one block.

Make the Cornerstones

Follow instructions under "Make Cornerstones" on page 161.

Make the Sashing Strips

Follow instructions under "Sashing Strips and Assembly" on page 161, # 1 thru # 7.

Complete the Pillow Top

See page 30 for layering and quilting. Then, follow the instructions on page 54 for making the Slip-cover Back. When complete, slide a pillow form inside and enjoy!

Make the Paws for Tablerunner

Refer to the photo of the finished table-runner on the previous page. Follow the instructions on pages 160-161 to make the needed bear paw squares. Make one block as you did for the pillow, and then add Bear Paws to each side.

Cutting for Tablerunner:

❖ Dark Fabrics A:
Cut the following from dark fabrics:
(24) 2-1/2" squares; (1) 2" square
(12) 3-1/2" squares

❖ Light Fabrics B:
Cut the following from light fabrics:
(2) 2" x 14" strips; (12) 2" squares
(2) 2" x 5" strips; (24) 2-1/2" squares
(3) 2-1/2" strips

Assemble the Blocks

1. See page 160 under Assemble the Blocks.
Make (12) of Unit A
Make (12) of Unit B
Make (12) of Unit C
Make (12) of Unit D
Make (12) of Unit E

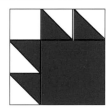

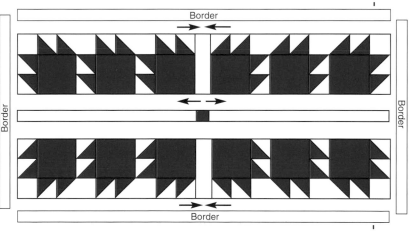

2. Add the 2-1/2" border strips. See Border instructions on page 163.

See page 28 for making a "Quilt Sandwich". Then refer to pages 30 - 33 for your favorite method of quilting.

See page 46 for binding.

Window Wonders

Block 1
Make 20 ▶

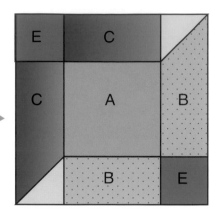

Credits:
Level: Beginner
Quilt designed & pieced by:
    Nancy Bryant
Quilted by:
    Evelyn Byler using Sulky Blendables
    #4013 Sun & Sea
Featured Fabric:
    Theme Fabric - Moda Waterlilies,
    Moda Fishy Folly, and Hoffman

Quilt Size: Approx. 69" x 71-1/2"

See the Christmas version
of this Quilt on page 170.

Fabrics & Supplies Needed for Quilt:

All strips are cut across the fabric, selvage to selvage,
assuming 42" of usable fabric. Cut off all selvages.

❖ 1 yd. Fabric A - Main theme print
❖ 1 yd. Fabric B - Bottom and Right Side strips
❖ 1 yd. Fabric C - Top and Left Side strips
❖ 3/4 yd. Fabric D - Accent - Inner borders
❖ 1-3/4 yds. Fabric E - Outer borders
❖ 7/8 yd. Fabric A - Binding
❖ 5 yds. (42") or 2-1/2 yds. (108") for backing
❖ Hobbs 20/80 Batting, at least 70" x 80"
❖ Sulky Cotton Blendables™ and Sulky Sliver™
❖ Machine needle size: 14/90 Topstitch
❖ General Sewing Supplies - see page 3

Cutting: Make a Fabric Key - page 8. Read page 5 before cutting.

❖ Fabric A: Main Theme Fabric
    Cut (4) 6-1/2" strips.

❖ Fabric B: Right and Bottom Strips
    Cut (9) 3-1/2" strips. Set four strips aside.
        From the remaining 5 strips, cut (20) 3-1/2" x 9-1/2" strips.

❖ Fabric C: Left and Top Strips
    Cut (9) 3-1/2" strips. Set four strips aside.
        From the remaining 5 strips, cut (20) 3-1/2" x 9-1/2" strips.

❖ Fabric D: Accent Inner Border
    Cut (8) 1-1/2" strips for the inner border.
    Cut (4) 3-1/2" strips. From these, cut (40) 3-1/2" squares.

❖ Fabric E: Part of Block and Outer Border
    Cut (8) 6" strips for the outer border.
    Cut (4) 3-1/2" strips. From these, cut (40) 3-1/2" squares.

Bell-Bryson Homeplace
Franklin, NC

Center Strip Set   Read page 6 before beginning to sew 1/4" seams.

1. Sew a 3-1/2" strip of fabrics B and C to each side of a 6-1/2" strip of fabric A to form a strip set as illustrated below.

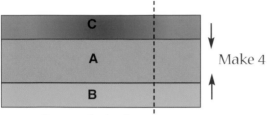

Make 4

Center Strip Set

2. Press seams toward the center.

3. Cut into (20) 6-1/2" segments.

Window Frames - Right

1. Draw a diagonal line from corner to corner on the wrong side of (20) of the 3-1/2" fabric "D" squares.

2. Place a 3-1/2" square of fabric "D" (with the drawn line), right sides together, on the end of a 3-1/2" x 9-1/2" strip of fabric "B" as illustrated below.

3. Stitch on the diagonal drawn line.

4. * Trim away the fabric 1/4" past the line of stitching as shown.

5. Flip and press the cut 3-1/2" square on the stitched line to form a triangle.

6. Sew a 3-1/2" square of fabric "E" to the other end.

7. Press seam toward the fabric "E"

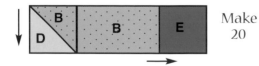

Make 20

★ The size of the rectangle must remain the same. Before trimming away the excess fabric in both #4's below, flip the triangle back and finger press. Make sure the edges of the triangle line up to the original edges of the rectangle. If desired for the sake of accuracy, trim away just the inside piece of fabric and leave the original rectangle intact. This technique is not suitable for hand quilting, as it adds too much bulk.

Window Frames - Left

1. Draw a diagonal line from corner to corner on the wrong side of the remaining (20) 3-1/2" fabric "D" squares.

2. Place a 3-1/2" square of fabric "D", right sides together, on the end of a 3-1/2" x 9-1/2" strip of fabric "C" as illustrated below.

3. Stitch on the drawn diagonal line.

4. * Trim away the fabric 1/4" past the line of stitching as shown below.

5. Flip and press the cut 3-1/2" square on the stitched line to form a triangle.

6. Add a 3-1/2" square of fabric "E" to the other end.

7. Press seam toward the fabric "E" square. Make 20 of these.

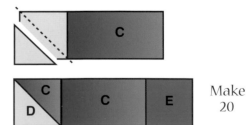

Make 20

Assemble the Block - Make 20

1. Add the fabric "B" side to the <u>right</u> of the 6-1/2" strip set.

2. Add the fabric "C" side to the <u>left</u> of the base strip set.

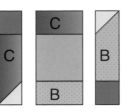

Make 20

3. Press the seams on *eight* of the blocks toward the *center square*, and the other *twelve* toward the *side sections*.

Assemble the Quilt Top

1. Make two four-block rows with the eight blocks that are *pressed toward the center*. Press seams to the left.

2. Make three four-block rows with the eight blocks that are *pressed toward the sides*. Press seams to the right.

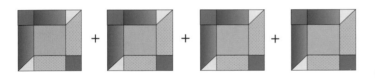

3. Assemble the top, alternating the rows so that the seams nest against one another.

Press toward:
Side

Center

Side

Center

Side

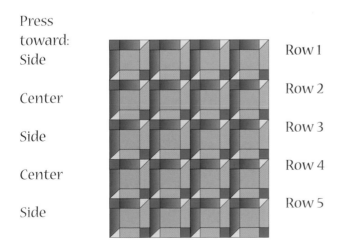

Row 1

Row 2

Row 3

Row 4

Row 5

Add Inner and Outer Borders
See Page 34.

Add a 1-1/2" inner and 6"outer border, as shown below.

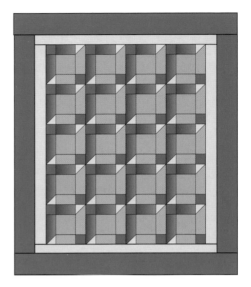

Layer Quilt - See page 28.

Quilting - See page 30.

Close up of quilting.
An overall design was used for the quilting pattern which was done on a long arm quilting machine using Sulky Multi-colored Blendables #4013.

Christmas Windows

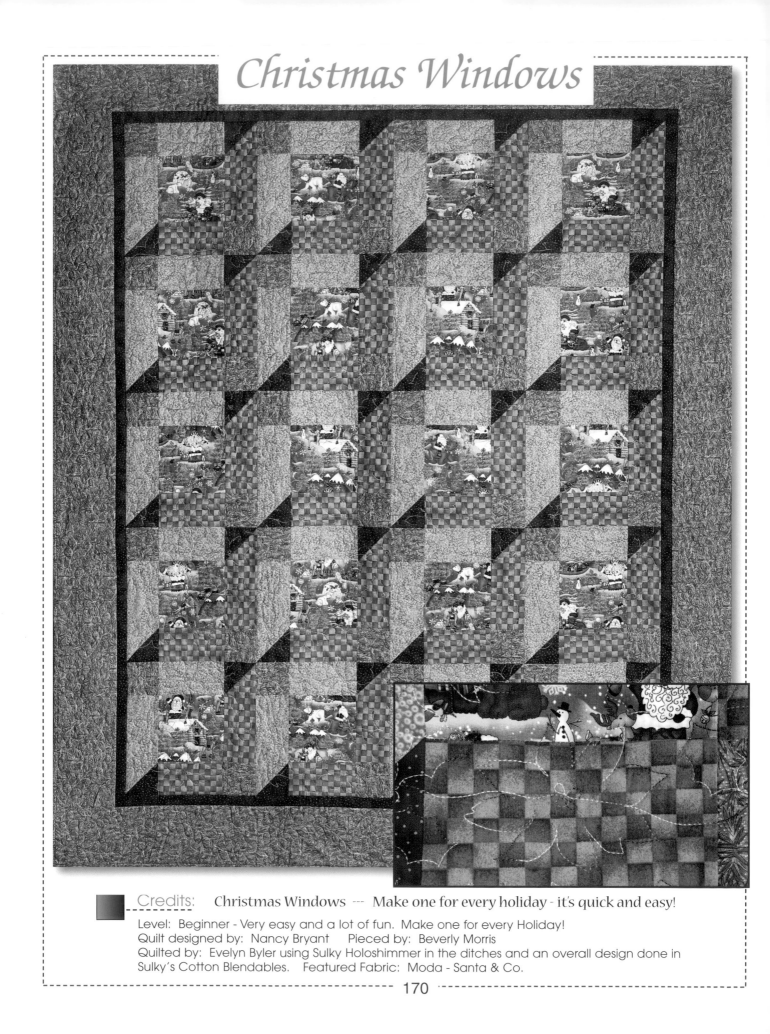

Credits: Christmas Windows --- *Make one for every holiday - it's quick and easy!*

Level: Beginner - Very easy and a lot of fun. Make one for every Holiday!
Quilt designed by: Nancy Bryant   Pieced by: Beverly Morris
Quilted by: Evelyn Byler using Sulky Holoshimmer in the ditches and an overall design done in Sulky's Cotton Blendables.   Featured Fabric: Moda - Santa & Co.

Triangle Triumph

This quilt is especially suited for featuring 4" embroidery designs or a theme fabric.

Credits:
Level: Advanced
Quilt designed by:
   Beverly Morris
Pieced by: Pam Laba
Quilted by: Evelyn Byler
Featured Fabrics: Scraps
Embroidery Featured:
   Redwork "Winter
   Woodlands" Collection 1

Quilt Size: Approx. 83" sq.

See it on page 172.

Fabrics and Supplies Needed for Quilt:

All strips are cut across the fabric, selvage to selvage, assuming 42" of usable fabric. Cut off all selvages.

❖ Fabric A - 1/3 yd. of 15 lights   ❖ Fabric B - 1/3 yd. of 15 darks
❖ Fabric C - 1-3/4 yd. of a light for center squares and triangles
❖ Fabric D - 3 yds. for 4-1/2" border and setting triangles
❖ Fabric E - 1-1/2 yds. of a light fabric for sashing   ❖ Fabric F - 3/4 yd. for bias binding
❖ Backing - 8 yds. (42") or 2-7/8 yds. (108")   ❖ Hobbs 20/80 Batting, at least 90" x 90"
❖ Embroidery Card GN-JD3 Winter Woodland Redwork Collection 1 by Joyce Drexler for
   Great Notions   ❖ Sulky 30 wt. Cotton Thread #1001 Bright White for piecing
❖ Sulky 12 wt. and 30 wt. Cotton #1071 Off White for quilting, and 30 wt. #1169 Bayberry
   Red for the embroideries   ❖ Machine needle: 14/90
❖ 18 sheets of Half-Square Triangle Paper, Finished Size: 2" (30 per sheet) to make a total
   of 520 half-square triangles   ❖ General sewing supplies - see page 3

Cutting: Read throughly before cutting. Label cut pieces. Make a Fabric Key - See page 8.

❖ Fabric A: Assorted lights for triangle paper -
   Cut (14) 10" x 15" pieces.

❖ Fabric B: Darks for triangles and cornerstones -
   Cut (14) 10" x 15" pieces. Combine with Fabric A and half-square triangle paper
   to make 520 half-square triangles. Cut (24) 2-1/2" squares for cornerstones.

❖ Fabric C: White center squares (or use a theme print) and triangles -
   Cut (4) 3" strips for triangles bordering the center square (if contrasting is desired).
   Cut (3) 6" strips. From these, cut (13) 6" squares.
      Note: If embroidering centers, cut (3) 8" strips. From these, cut (13)
      8" squares and trim them to 6" squares after embroidering.

❖ Fabric D: Setting triangles and borders -
      Cut (2) 28" squares. Cut these in half diagonally, twice, to make the 8
   setting triangles. Cut (2) 14" squares for the corner triangles. Cut these in half
   diagonally to make (4) triangles. See additional information on setting triangles
   on pages 9 and 26. Cut (10) 4-1/2" strips.

❖ Fabric E: Sashing - Cut (3) 16-1/2" strips. From these, cut (36) 2-1/2" x 16-1/2" strips.

❖ Fabric F: Binding - Cut (9) 2-1/2" strips. See page 36.

Credits:

Level: Advanced
Quilt pieced by:
Sharon Stokes
Featured Fabric: Hoffman
Featured Embroidery Card:
"Winter Woodlands" Collection 2
(filled) by Joyce Drexler

Begin to sew the Block

1. Sew together most of the half-square triangles as shown below. Be sure to have the dark sides facing as shown. If using 15 different fabrics, mix them up for a great scrappy look.

Set "A" - Make 104
Press 52 to Light and 52 to Dark.

Set "B" - Make 104
Press 52 to Light and 52 to Dark.

2. Sew together into square units as shown below. Make 52 of Unit A and 52 of Unit B.

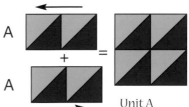

Unit A
Make 52

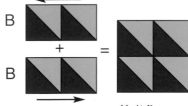

Unit B
Make 52

3. Sew a Unit A to a Unit B to make a larger Unit C. Make 52.

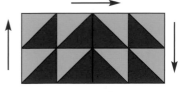

Unit C - Make 52

Additional Cutting Required

Note: If you intend to do embroidery in the featured centers of the (13) 6" squares, start by cutting (13) 8" squares of fabric C. Stabilize properly and embroider the center of each piece. Center the design and trim down to (13) 6" squares, then remove the stabilizer. (Blocks can be embroidered on point if desired.)

❖ **Light Fabric A**
Cut (4) 5-1/2" strips. Cut these into (26) 5-1/2" squares. Cut these squares diagonally to make 52 triangles.

❖ **Dark Fabric B**
Cut (4) 3" strips. Cut these into (52) 3" squares. Cut these squares diagonally to make 104 triangles.

❖ **Light Fabric C**
Cut (4) 3" strips from the same fabric that you have cut the 6" squares (or 8" if embroidering center). Cut these into (52) 3" squares. Cut these squares diagonally to make 104 triangles.

Continue Sewing the Block

1. Sew two of the dark fabric triangles to one of the remaining 2-1/2" half-square triangles to make a Unit D. Make 52.

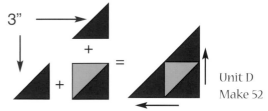

Unit D
Make 52

2. Sew a 5-1/2" triangle to a Unit D to make a Unit E. Make 52.

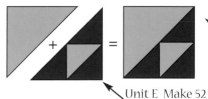

Trim unit to 4-1/2" square.
See trimming instructions on page 10.

Unit E Make 52

3. Attach a Unit E to both ends of a rectangular Unit C to form a Unit F. Make 26.

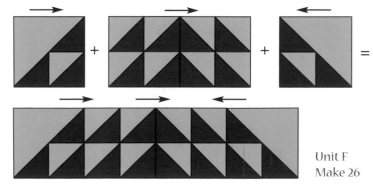

Unit F
Make 26

173

4. Sew 2 of the light Fabric C triangles to one of the remaining 2-1/2" half-square triangles to make a Unit G. Make 52.

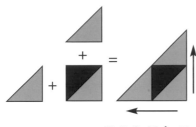

Unit G - Make 52

5. Attach a Unit G to each of the 4 sides of a 6" light square (or an 8" embroidered square that is trimmed to 6") to make a Unit H. Press toward triangles. Make 13.

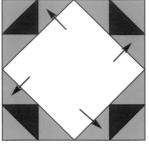

Unit H - Make 13

6. Sew a Unit C to both sides of a Unit H as illustrated below to make a Unit J. Make 13.

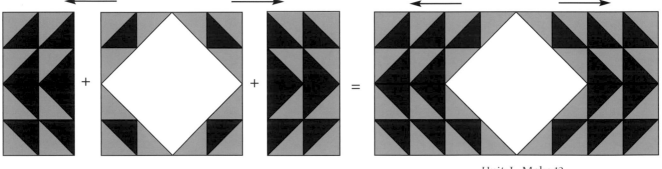

Unit J - Make 13

7. Sew a rectangular Unit F to the top and bottom of a Unit J to make a Unit K block. Make 13.

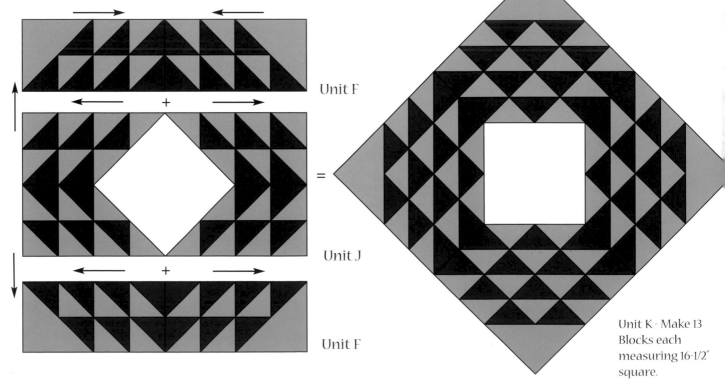

Unit F

Unit J

Unit F

Unit K - Make 13 Blocks each measuring 16-1/2" square.

174

Add the Sashing and Cornerstones to the Blocks.
See the layout on the next page for reference.

1. Sew a 2-1/2" square of Fabric B to each end of a 2-1/2" x 16-1/2" Sashing Fabric Strip E. Press toward the sashing.   Make 8.

Sashing strip with 2 squares added. Make 8.

2. Sew a 2-1/2" square of Fabric B to one end of a 2-1/2" x 16-1/2" Sashing Strip Fabric E. Press toward the sashing.   Make 8 sets.

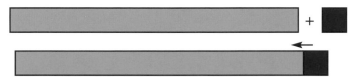

Sashing strip with 1 square added. Make 8.

Note:

If you have embroidered the 6" squares, be sure that they are all facing in the proper direction before sewing the rows together.

Sew Rows in sequence as shown in the layout on the next page.

1. Lay out the blocks and sashing strips on a flat surface. (See note above right.)

2. Sew row 1 as shown. Press seams toward the sashing. Continue sewing each row until all 7 rows are completed. Then, sew each row to one another until you have your quilt top completed. Press to the sashing.

Credits:

Level: Advanced
Quilt designed and pieced by:
   Carol Ingram
Featured Fabric: Black and White
   Collection
Thread: Sulky Blendable #4007
Featured Embroidery Card:
   "Fashion Hats" by Carol Ingram
   for "Inspira" Designs™
   (see www.husqvarnaviking.com)

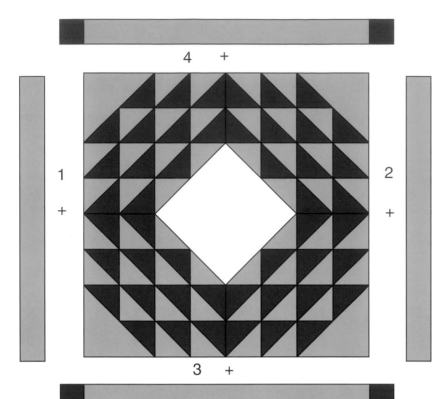

4 +

1
+

2
+

3 +

Finishing

Read more about Setting and Corner Triangles on pages 10 and 11.

Note: Triangles will be larger than needed. Trim to size after piecing leaving 1/4" seam allowance all around.

Read general directions for Layering, Backing and adding Borders and Binding starting on page 26.

Note: Always measure through the center of the quilt and cut border strips to that measurement.

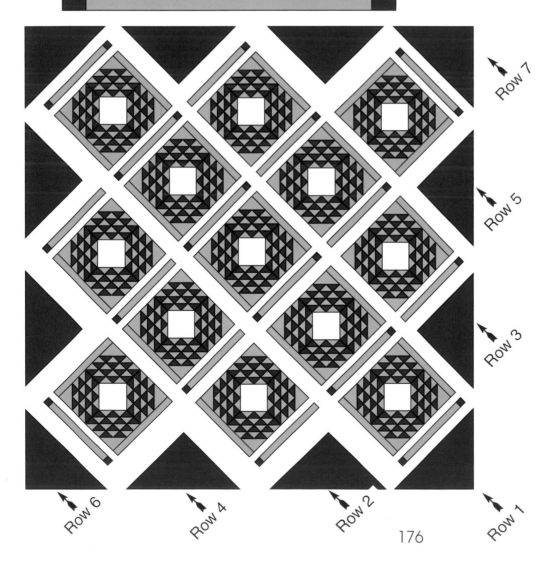

Row 7

Row 5

Row 3

Row 6

Row 4

Row 2

Row 1